TS4601

Brecht's Plays, Poetry and Prose
annotated and edited in hardback and paperback
by John Willett and Ralph Manheim
Methuen London publish all titles. Methuen New York only those marked †

Collected Plays

Vol. 1	Baal; Drums in the Night; In the Jungle of Cities; The Life
(*hardback*	of Edward II of England; A Respectable Wedding; The
only)	Beggar; Driving Out a Devil; Lux in Tenebris; The Catch
Vol. 1i	Baal (*paperback only*)
Vol. 1ii	A Respectable Wedding and other one-act plays (*paperback only*)
Vol. 1iii	Drums in the Night (*paperback only*)
Vol. 1iv	In the Jungle of Cities (*paperback only*)
Vol. 2i	Man equals Man; The Elephant Calf
Vol. 2ii	The Threepenny Opera
Vol. 2iii	The Rise and Fall of the City of Mahagonny; The Seven Deadly Sins
*Vol. 3i	Saint Joan of the Stockyards
*Vol. 3ii	The Baden-Baden Cantata; The Flight over the Ocean; He Who Said Yes; He Who Said No; The Decision
*Vol. 4i	The Mother; The Exception and the Rule; The Horatii and the Curiatii
*Vol. 4ii	Round Heads and Pointed Heads
*Vol. 4iii	Señora Carrar's Rifles; Fear and Misery of the Third Reich
Vol. 5i	Life of Galileo
Vol. 5ii	Mother Courage and her Children
*Vol. 5iii	The Trial of Lucullus; Dansen; What's the Price of Iron?
*Vol. 6i	The Good Person of Szechwan
Vol. 6ii	The Resistible Rise of Arturo Ui
*Vol. 6iii	Mr Puntila and his Man Matti
Vol. 7	The Visions of Simone Machard; Schweyk in the Second World War; The Caucasian Chalk Circle; The Duchess of Malfi
*Vol. 8i	The Days of the Commune
*Vol. 8ii	Turandot; Report from Herrenburg
*Vol. 8iii	Downfall of the Egoist Johann Fatzer; The Life of Confucius; The Breadshop; The Salzburg Dance of Death

Poetry
† Poems 1913–1956

Prose
Brecht on Theatre
Diaries 1920–1922
† Short Stories 1921–1946
*Selected Essays

Also
† Happy End (by Brecht, Weill and Lane)

*in preparation

The following plays are also available (in paperback only) in unannotated editions:
The Caucasian Chalk Circle; The Days of the Commune; The Good Person
of Szechwan; The Life of Galileo; The Measures Taken and other
Lehrstücke; The Messingkauf Dialogues; Mr. Puntila and his Man Matti;
The Mother; Saint Joan of the Stockyards

Happy End

A melodrama with songs

Lyrics by Bertolt Brecht

Music by Kurt Weill

Original German play by
Dorothy Lane

Translated, adapted and introduced by
Michael Feingold

T54601

Methuen · London and New York

First published in Great Britain simultaneously in hardback and as a Methuen Paperback in 1982 by Methuen London Ltd, 11 New Fetter Lane, London EC4P 4EE

First published in the United States of America simultaneously in hardback and paperback by Methuen Inc, 733 Third Avenue, New York, NY 10017

ISBN 0 413 50950 8 (Hardback)
     0 413 51020 4 (Paperback)

Printed in Great Britain by
Richard Clay (The Chaucer Press) Ltd, Bungay, Suffolk

Library of Congress Cataloging in Publication Data

Weill, Kurt, 1900–1950.
  Happy end.
  Libretto to the musical play, translated from the German.
  Text by Btecht, music by Weill.
  "The story was [originally] credited to a mythical 'Dorothy Lane' "—Pref.
  1. Music revues, comedies, etc.—Librettos.
I. Brecht, Bertolt, 1898–1956. II. Title.
ML50.W42H42 1982   782.81'2   82–12553
ISBN 0-413-50950-8
ISBN 0-413-51020-4 (pbk.)

Introduction

In 1928, the young writer-composer team of Bertolt Brecht and Kurt Weill had reached the height of its pre-war fame. The success of *The Threepenny Opera* had converted Brecht, the outspoken avant-garde poet, and Weill, the intensely serious modernist composer, into Brecht-&-Weill, the clever musical comedy duo whose smash hit (within a year of its opening *Threepenny Opera* had received over thirty European productions) had the whole continent whistling its seductive pop tunes and quoting its cynical couplets.

This kind of middlebrow popular success actually sat rather awkwardly on the two men, and the fallout from *Threepenny* left both of them preoccupied with more serious projects. Brecht, who had recently embraced Marx's economic theories, was working on his giant capitalist tragedy *St Joan of the Stockyards*, while Weill had returned to his most ambitious theatre project to date, the full-length opera *Rise and Fall of the City of Mahagonny*, the composition of which had been interrupted by the hasty execution of *Threepenny* shortly after Brecht finished drafting the libretto (expanded from the 1926 *Mahagonny Songplay* or 'Little' *Mahagonny*, their first collaboration). For the moment, they thought, they were through with the commercial theatre.

That they were not is due to the persistence of one man, the ebullient producer Ernst Josef Aufricht, who was not about to let the sources of his huge *Threepenny* success get away so easily. Aufricht proposed that, for the fall of 1929, Brecht and Weill write him a contemporary sequel to *Threepenny Opera* (which had been based on John Gay's 18th-century *Beggar's Opera*, updated by Brecht to Queen Victoria's time), to be produced with the same cast, at the same theatre in Berlin (the cosy Schiffbauerdamm, now the home of the Berliner Ensemble), opening on the first anniversary of *Threepenny*'s memorable opening night.

The promise of redoubled fame and fortune made Aufricht's offer hard to resist, and Brecht quickly started casting about for a suitable story to adapt. Elisabeth Hauptmann, his faithful secretary, had the answer, discovered in the course of her exhaustive English-language reading (she was the one who had translated *The Beggar's Opera*, after its triumphant London revival by Nigel Playfair, and proposed it to Brecht in the first place). To this day no one is certain exactly what Hauptmann's English source was; to avoid copyright problems the story was credited to a mythical 'Dorothy Lane' and described as having appeared in the non-existent 'J. & L. Weekly, St. Louis'. The similarity to the plot of *Guys and Dolls* has led many to speculate that Damon Runyon was the source of *Happy End*. Unfortunately for them Runyon's story, 'The Idyll of Miss Sarah Brown', from which Frank Loesser's musical is drawn, didn't appear in print till the early 1930s.

A romance between a Salvation Army worker and a street tough, however, was no surprise in the fictional conventions of the time. Bernard Shaw, one of Brecht's early idols, had opened up the stage possibilities of the material in *Major Barbara* (1905), in which the aristocratic Barbara has an intense confrontation with a surly dockside labourer, Bill Walker (note the similarity to the name Bill Cracker). And *Major Barbara*, reset in Chicago with details lifted from Upton Sinclair's *The Jungle*, was Brecht's starting point for *St Joan of the Stockyards*. Another likely source was Edward Sheldon's *Salvation Nell* (1909), an early triumph of the American realist movement led by the popular actress Minnie Maddern Fiske, who made a huge success in the central role of a goodhearted slum girl, saved by Army preaching, who struggles to rescue her common-law husband from gin and fisticuffs. One of Nell's cohorts is a popular hellfire preacher nicknamed Hallelujah Maggie, and the first act is set in a saloon on Christmas Eve.

Brecht and Hauptmann, in any case, embroidered freely on whatever they took from their unidentified source or sources, inventing with their politics, their complex European vision of America, and the specific abilities of their actors in mind. A sinister Oriental modelled on the silent film roles of Sessue Haya-kawa was an obvious role for Peter Lorre, who had worked well with Brecht at Munich in *In the Jungle of Cities*; a gangster who robbed banks in women's clothes, improbably, was an amusing one for the portly Kurt Gerron, who had made a hit as Tiger Brown. Carola Neher, who had given up the lead role of Polly Peachum in *Threepenny* at the last moment to be at her dying husband's bedside, would play the heroic Salvation Army lass, while the gang would be filled out with two Brechtian favourites, Oscar Homolka (who had played the name part in *Baal* and Mortimer in *Edward II*) and Theo Lingen (who had given a memorable performance as the Clown in the *Badener Lehrstück* the year before).

Actors whose old-fashioned attitudes had caused clashes with Brecht in *Threepenny* rehearsals were quietly passed over: The slick operetta tenor Harald Paulsen (Macheath, who later rejoined the team for *Mahagonny*), the cabaret *diseuse* Rosa Valletti (who had refused to sing Mrs Peachum's 'filthy' song about sexual slavery), the stodgy Erich Ponto (Peachum) were not to be seen in *Happy End*. Most notable of the omissions was Kurt Weill's wife, Lotte Lenya, whose performance as Jenny had made her the toast of Berlin. Her absence, however, was not due to Brecht but to the enterprise of Moritz Seeler, director of the prestigious Berliner Volksbühne's *Junge Bühne*, or second stage, which had signed her for an adventurous season that included *Danton's Death* (Lenya played Lucile Desmoulins) and the still scandalous *Spring Awakening* (Lorre, joining the company after *Happy End* closed, played a memorable Moritz Stiefel to her Ilse).

Brecht's wife, however, was definitely present. Helene Weigel, whom he had recently married and who shared both his new Communist beliefs and his aesthetic militancy, was cast as the Lady in Grey. She had regarded *Threepenny Opera* (in which she played the small role of the brothel madam) as a severely compromised work from a political point of view, and was determined to see that no such compromise afflicted *Happy End*. It hardly needs to be said that this was not what Aufricht and his crew had in mind. The script had turned out to be a jolly escapist romp with a few leftist gibes along the way, its acid undercurrent getting lost in the 'collaborative' bedlam that accompanied any Brecht rehearsal, and Weigel apparently grew more and more dissatisfied.

Accounts of what actually took place on the opening night of *Happy End* (2 September 1929 – exactly a year and two days after the opening of *Threepenny*) differ markedly. We know that the first two acts passed without incident, and were favourably received. Years later, Lenya remembered Weill telephoning her backstage at intermission, to say he was sure they had a hit. The third act, however, was marred by a fatal incident: The Lady in Grey's final speech, which seems harmless enough in the text as it stands, aroused violent booing and whistling from the expensive seats, which in turn stimulated shouts and counter-arguments from the gallery, precipitating a near-riot. Some assert that Brecht had rewritten Weigel's speech privately with intent to provoke, others that she improvised a diatribe against capitalism, still others that she pulled a notorious Communist Party broad-side from the pocket of her costume and began to harangue the audience with excerpts from it.

Whatever the source of the provocation, the middle-class part of the audience was duly provoked, and, to make matters worse, Brecht and director Erich Engel had contrived to follow the speech with an ironic hymn to capitalism (now traditionally used as the Prologue) which called for the emergence on stage of mock stained-glass windows representing Saint Rockefeller, Saint Henry Ford, and Saint J. P. Morgan. To a German bour-geois audience with a sizeable respect for both religion and money, this was the last straw, and the first-nighters responded with yells, threats, and what one reviewer described as a 'concert of whistling'. The critics, barely escaping with their dignity intact, gave Brecht and company a thorough belabouring in the next day's papers, with B.B.'s arch-enemy, the staid and influential Alfred Kerr, mocking the work's derivations with the phrase *'Happy entlehnt'* ('happily borrowed' – it was Kerr who had accused Brecht of plagiarizing Villon in the *Threepenny* lyrics), and suggesting that Engel would do better to write plays himself than to get them from such as Brecht. The other critics followed Kerr's lead, with even Brecht's loyal supporter Herbert Jhering complaining that the last tableau appeared to belong to an entirely different play. (He was not far from wrong: Its lyric, along with several other key sections of *Happy End*, turned up the next year in *St. Joan of the Stockyards*.) The ticket-buying public, dismayed by the notices and fearful of riots, shunned the work, which closed two days later, an ignominious failure.

Brecht subsequently repudiated the script, crediting it in his notes on *St. Joan* entirely to Hauptmann. When it was finally revived in 1958, she followed suit, instructing the German publisher to use only the name 'Dorothy Lane' on the title page.

They were right to do so; the original version, despite some amusing moments, is a desperately casual makeshift, which just happens to serve as a dramatic setting for some of the greatest theatre songs ever written. The present version is a free adaptation, which treats the 'Dorothy Lane' script as loosely as the collaborators of 1929 treated their mysterious source. Only the lyrics, whose authorship Brecht never denied, have been kept in more or less literal translation.

If *Happy End* was a setback for Brecht, for Weill it was a pure victory. The songs, as interpreted by Lenya and countless other artists, are among the keystones of his reputation, and have kept the idea of the show alive even when its script seemed totally unfeasible. Over the years, the score has served as a sort of reservoir from which people could draw music for other Kurt Weill shows: 'The Bilbao Song', in New York, was interpolated into the off-Broadway *Threepenny Opera*, Anglicized by Marc Blitzstein as 'Our Bide-a-Wee in Soho'. The lyric of the 'Mandalay Song' was given a new setting by Weill for the 'Loving' scene of *Mahagonny*, and several of the Salvation Army hymns turned up in Weill's Paris musical, *Marie Galante*, four years later, as decidedly profane French dance-hall tunes, with 'In Our Childhood's Bright Endeavour' becoming 'The Young Girls of Bordeaux'. Since the current adaptation was commissioned by Robert Brustein's Yale Repertory Theatre in 1972, numerous American productions have been given, with a Broadway production (featuring former Yale Rep actors Meryl Streep and Christopher Lloyd) spearheading the Kurt Weill revival that subsequently engulfed New York. *Happy End* in its latest incarnation has found its way to Australia and Wales, to British repertory companies and American resident theatres, to universities, and to London's West End in 1975 in a production by the Oxford Playhouse. Despite its stormy beginnings, *Happy End* is now thriving, to use a word Brecht coined for the occasion, *happyendlich*.

MICHAEL FEINGOLD

Happy End

A Melodrama with Songs

Characters

The Gang:
BILL CRACKER
SAM 'MAMMY' WURLITZER
DR. NAKAMURA ('THE GOVERNOR')
JIMMY DEXTER ('THE REVEREND')
BOB MARKER ('THE PROFESSOR')
JOHNNY FLINT ('BABY FACE')
A LADY IN GREY ('THE FLY')
MIRIAM, *the barmaid*

The Salvation Army:
MAJOR STONE, *female*
CAPTAIN HANNIBAL JACKSON
LIEUTENANT LILLIAN HOLIDAY ('HALLELUJAH LIL')
SISTER MARY
SISTER JANE
BROTHER BEN OWENS

Also:
A COP
Members of the fold

Place: Chicago
Time: December 1919

Prologue

Limbo. The entire Company huddle together in a tight group. Only faces visible. Slides: The portraits of presidents on dollar bills blown up huge and tinted like the pictures of saints on stained-glass windows. Alternative: Giant stained-glass caricatures of St. Henry Ford, St. John D. Rockefeller, and St. J. P. Morgan.

COMPANY *sing*:

> Praise to the Fords and Rockefellers – Hosannah!
> The buyers and the sellers – Hosannah!
> Give them the City and the State – Hosannah!
> Hosannah! Hosannah! Hosannah! Hosannah!

Blackout. Music changes to a raucous foxtrot. The slides, moving in tempo with the music, change to a series of stills of the cast in costume, with the character's name and the actor's name superimposed on them, in the style of old movie credits. The series opens with: 'The management of this theatre proudly presents HAPPY END, by Bertolt Brecht and Kurt Weill,' *and, when the entire cast has been shown, changes to authentic period photographs of Chicago, emphasizing the poor, the Salvation Army, wealthy people on Michigan Avenue, crowded slums, etc. Over the last of these, just as the Prologue music ends, is projected the title:* CHICAGO/DECEMBER 1919. *In the second of silence between the Prologue and Act One, a new title is flashed on the screen by itself:* BILL'S BEER HALL – A WAY STATION ON THE ROAD TO HELL.

Act One

Bill's Beer Hall. Late afternoon. Winter. A bar with a row of stools. Pianola to one side. Prominent on the other wall, a hatrack with many hats on it. Exit to back room behind bar. A view of the street outside, possibly a flight of steps leading to it.

It is late afternoon outside, but the bar-room is dimly lit. Miriam is at the bar, washing glasses, tough, disinterested. The Professor is seated in a chair downstage centre, wearing a hat, coat, and scarf. He has a false moustache on and affects a thick German accent. He is writhing in the glare of a high-intensity lantern held by the Reverend. Baby Face stands menacingly over him wearing brass knuckles. Sam looks on anxiously nearby, and Dr. Nakamura watches from upstage, hidden in the semi-darkness.

PROFESSOR *getting up, as if trying to escape*: Pliss –

BABY FACE *pushing him back down*: Siddown, Kraut!

PROFESSOR: But mine vife und children –

BABY FACE: Siddown, I said, or I'll ram dese brass knuckles down yer troat!

SAM: Now hold on there, Baby Face. We can treat the gentleman better than that, can't we?

BABY FACE: Well, he ain't been treatin' us so good, and I'm fed up. He's gonna get his face bashed in.

SAM *jumping in between Baby Face and the Professor*: No, don't hurt him! He didn't mean to do us dirt. He's a nice guy. Aren't you, Mr. Prinzmeyer?

PROFESSOR: Pliss – I haff a vife and children – pliss –

SAM: You see, he's a nice guy. He'll play along. The Governor's gonna give him another chance, wait and see. What do you say, Governor?

PROFESSOR: Pliss –

GOVERNOR (DR. NAKAMURA) *from the darkness*: He have been warn three time already.

BABY FACE: Lemme at him!

SAM: No, Baby Face! Governor, I appeal to you. Give the fellow a break. He's a good man. Why, he's even an Elk.

GOVERNOR *coming forward*: Step out of way, Sammy. Mr. Pharmacist Prinzmeyer, I will explain once again: Do you wish your drugstore be protected from criminals?

PROFESSOR: Ja – ja.

GOVERNOR: If you want protection, you must to pay us every month. Otherwise, who know what may transpire?

PROFESSOR: But I haff told you, I haff no money. Mein vife is ein zick voman. Pliss –

GOVERNOR: Do not trifle with us, Mr. Pharmacist. Is unwise. Have you ever heard of – The Fly?

PROFESSOR: Vot – vot iss der Fly?

GOVERNOR: If you miss payment, Mr. Prinzmeyer, will come a day when mysterious woman in grey stop you on street and ask for light for her cigarette. That is signal, Mr. Prinzmeyer. From that moment, you are marked man. When you light cigarette for The Fly, flame of your life soon snuffed out.

PROFESSOR *weeping*: Nein, nein.

GOVERNOR: Reverend! Please to show our friend hat collection!

The lantern that has been aimed at the Professor's face swivels to the hatrack, wobbles.

GOVERNOR: A little higher, Reverend.

REVEREND: Sorry, Governor. This contraption's awfully hot.

The Professor squirms in his chair, starting to say something.

BABY FACE: Siddown, you!

GOVERNOR: Do you see hats on wall, Mr. Prinzmeyer? They have been collected by our friend Bill Cracker. Do you know him?

The lantern wobbles again.

GOVERNOR: Higher, Reverend.

REVEREND: Extremely sorry.

GOVERNOR: When he hang hat so high in air, head that once wore hat six feet underground. Care to see your hat on rack, Mr. Prinzmeyer?

PROFESSOR: Nein – nein.

GOVERNOR: Then think again, please. Will you pay to us, or no? Let us read answer on Mr. Prinzmeyer's face, Reverend.

The light does not move.

GOVERNOR: Light, Reverend.

The light does not move.

GOVERNOR: Reverend!

REVEREND: I'm sorry. I can't hold that infernal thing a minute longer!

PROFESSOR *ripping off false moustache*: Dummy, why don't you grip it the way I showed you?

As the Professor gets up and starts arguing with the Reverend about the lantern, Baby Face tries to make him sit back down and Sam tries to make all of them go back into the scene. Three counts of ad libbed bedlam.

GOVERNOR *topping the bedlam*: Stop! Silence. Light, Miriam. *Miriam switches on the bar lights. Everyone relaxes – we see that it's only a rehearsal.*

GOVERNOR: We do it one more time, gentlemen. And this time we get it right.

PROFESSOR: Can we take a break first? That light's killin' my eyes.

REVEREND: If you'd put a handle on that damn reflector –

PROFESSOR: If you'd just hold it the way I showed ya –

REVEREND: I have better things to worry about than your metallic imbecilities.

The Professor starts to answer back; the Governor interrupts him.

GOVERNOR *sharply*: We have all to worry about this. Prinzmeyer is president of Mercantile Association. If he refuse to pay us protection, they will all refuse. We cannot countenance rebellion.

SAM: I got a new idea. If you can work out a way to send them out of the room and let me talk to him alone –

GOVERNOR: Is too complicated –

SAM: – then I can work in my organ as a compromise offer.

GOVERNOR: Organ??

SAM: That church organ we picked up in the St. Luke's job last month. I ain't found a way of unloading it yet. I'll get old Prinzmeyer to buy it on time – that's how we'll get the payments out of him –

GOVERNOR *cutting Sam off, somewhere around 'on time'*: Sam! *Sam quickly shuts up.* Please to keep your organ out of shakedown operation. This serious business. *He sees Miriam going to the Professor with a cloth for his eyes, takes it away from her and throws it at the Professor.* Beer, Miriam.

Miriam silently draws a beer and brings it to the Governor. As he takes it from her, the Reverend pinches her fanny. She turns on him angrily, but decides not to say anything and goes back behind the bar. Men laugh.

PROFESSOR *throwing the cloth back at Miriam*: Oh boy, Jimmy. You wouldn't do that if Bill was here.

BABY FACE: Where is Bill, anyways?

PROFESSOR: Yeah, we need him for this job, ya know.

REVEREND: That's right. Our threats won't mean diddly-squat if we can't back them up.

PROFESSOR: So when is Bill gettin' back?

BABY FACE *overlapping*: Yeah, what's takin' him so long?

REVEREND *overlapping at the same time*: Yes, he'd better be here soon.

GOVERNOR *cutting them off*: Gentlemen, please! Mr. Cracker will be back today. If not, he will be replace tomorrow. In any case work will proceed. Fly has ordered.

Thud of a newspaper hitting the front door All duck, the Governor motions to Baby Face, who cautiously goes to the door.

BABY FACE: Hey, da paper's here. *All relax. He brings the paper in.* I got dibs on the funnies. *Unfolding the paper, he glances at the headline.* Hey, look at this: 'BAXLEY GANG ROBS TRAIN.'

Everyone reacts. Baby Face reads.

BABY FACE: 'Niagara Falls, New York – special dispatch. Concerned citizens looked on in horror yesterday evening as the infamous "Gorilla" Basley gang robbed the Chicago–Buffalo express train of over twenty thousand dollars in cash and gold bull-lion.'

By this time all are on their feet and moving towards Baby Face. On 'twenty thousand dollars' they all stop dead, in unison.

SAM: Twenty thousand dollars!

PROFESSOR: Wait till Bill hears about this!

BABY FACE *and* REVEREND *who is now looking over Baby's shoulder*: Sh! 'This gang of bullies further outraged respectability continued on page fourteen.'

BABY FACE: Huh?

REVEREND: Well, turn it, lunkhead!

Baby Face turns page. All are now clustered around paper.

BABY FACE *and others*: 'by boarding the train at Niagara Falls depot disguised as a wedding party. This mockery of the Christian sacrament was compounded by the repulsive Baxley himself being costumed as the bride. It is time, surely, for a new reign of law and order.'

SAM: Twenty thousand dollars!

BABY FACE: Bill's gonna explode!

PROFESSOR: He hates Baxley's guts anyway.

REVEREND: Baxley, Baxley, Baxley. Why don't *we* get breaks like that?

GOVERNOR: Calm, gentlemen. Our turn yet to come.

REVEREND: Sure, like Christmas.

NAKAMURA: Do not mock, Reverend. Important news arrive soon.

SAM: That's right, the Fly said we had a big job coming up.

REVEREND: Well, we knew her idea of a big job – shaking down some kraut druggist for six bits and a bottle of Sloan's Liniment. I ask you, what kind of professional crime is that?

GOVERNOR *firmly*: Promote calm on troubled water, Reverend.

REVEREND: Calm? This gang is so calm it's got rigor mortis. You'd think it was impossible for a crook to earn a decent living. But it's not: Look at Gorilla Baxley. I have to admire a man like that, even if he is our competition. He has enterprise; he aims high. And as my sainted mother used to say, a man who aims high is a great man. Not some penny-pushing gunslinger like our Bill. Gorilla Baxley is a great man. Gorilla Baxley is ambitious, Gorilla Baxley is imaginative, Gorilla Baxley is –

BILL *who has come in unobserved during this; he is holding a battered homburg, his face is bruised*: Dead.

EVERYONE: Bill!!

Title on screen: BILL CRACKER – HIS TOUGH EXTERIOR CONCEALED A HEART OF STONE. *Bill goes to the hatrack and hangs the homburg with the other hats. He takes a piece of chalk from his pocket, and chalks above the hat the initials G.B.*

BILL: That's time for you, Reverend. Yesterday a great man – today a small erasure in the Book of Life.

The gang crowds over to shake Bill's hand and ad lib congratulations. Miriam throws him the keys to the bar.

BILL: Thanks, sweetheart.

GOVERNOR: A fine achievement, Bill. Congratulations. *Pulls him downstage, away from the others.* Fly isn't going to like this at all.

BILL: Stick the Fly. I can handle her. I can handle the both of youse. *He breaks away from the Governor and goes up to the bar.*

GOVERNOR *to everyone*: My friends, appropriate to celebrate. With Gorilla out of way, Chicago ours to run. Bill's Beer Hall will be centre of underworld.

BABY FACE: Awright!

GOVERNOR: It will be greatest place since original Bill's Beer Hall in Bilbao.

BABY FACE: I never heard of it.

GOVERNOR: Have you got a nickel?

BABY FACE: Sure.

GOVERNOR: Then I tell you all about it. *Puts nickel into the pianola, which lights up.* I don't remember all words, but Bill can help out.

BILL: Thanks, but no thanks.

Bill sits at the bar, turning his back to the Governor. Title: THE BILBAO SONG.

GOVERNOR *sings*:

Bill's Beer Hall in Bilbao, Bilbao, Bilbao
Was the most fantastic place I've ever known.
For just a dollar you'd get all you wanted, all you
    wanted, all you wanted
Of whatever kind of joy you called your own.

But if you had been around to join the fun
Well, I don't know if you'd have liked what you'd
    have seen:
The stools at the bar were damp with rye.
On the dance floor the grass grew high.
Through the roof the moon was shining green.

And the music really gave you some return on what
    you paid.
(Hey, Joe play that old song they always played!)
    That old Bilbao moon
    Down where we used to go
Speaking:
Who remembers the words?
Singing:
    That old Bilbao moon
Speaking:
It's just too long ago!
Singing:
    I don't know if
    It would have brought you joy or grief
    But
    It was fantastic
    It was fantastic
    It was fantastic
    Beyond belief!

BABY FACE:

Bill's Beer Hall in Bilbao, Bilbao, Bilbao
Came a day the end of May in nineteen-eight
Four guys from Frisco came with bags of gold dust,
    bags of gold dust, bags of gold dust
And the time they showed us all was really great!

But if you had been around to see the fun, well,
I don't know if you'd have liked what you'd have seen:
The brandy bottles smashing everywhere
And the chairs flying through the air
– Through the roof the moon still shining green
'N those four guys all going crazy, with their pistols
    blazing high.
Think you can stop 'em? well, go right ahead and try!

That old Bilbao moon
Speaking:
Can't remember the words
Singing:
That old Bilbao moon
Speaking:
Something with 'love' in it
Singing:
   I don't know if
   It would have brought you joy or grief
   But
   It was fantastic
   It was fantastic
   It was fantastic
   Beyond belief!

BILL *turning around*: Awright, I got a good one for yez!
Sings:

Bill's Beer Hall in Bilbao, Bilbao, Bilbao
Now they've cleaned it up and made it middle-class
With potted palms and ice cream, very bourgeois, very
   bourgoeis
Just another place to put your ass!

But if you should come around to see the fun
Well, I don't know, you might not find it such a pain
   (Huh!)

They've mopped up all the booze and broken glass.
On parquet floors you can't grow grass.
They shut the green moon out because of rain.
And the music makes you cringe now, when you think
   of what you paid.
(Hey, Joe, play that old song they always played!)

Bill shouts the lyrics between phrases, and the others pick them up and sing them. It's obvious that he's the only one who knows the song.

EVERYBODY:

> That old Bilbao Moon
> Down where we used to go
> That old Bilbao moon
> Casting its golden glow
> That old Bilbao moon
> Love never laid me low
> That old Bilbao moon
> Why does it haunt me so?
>
> I don't know if
> It would have brought you joy or grief
> But
> It was fantastic
> It was fantastic
> It was fantastic
> Beyond belief!

BILL *spoken:* And it's all over now!

The sentimental lighting that has come up on them for the song suddenly fades. Lights up very bright on the street. A Lady in Grey enters. The Cop catches her and carries her into the saloon. Title on screen: A MYSTERIOUS GUEST!! *Projection: A housefly.*

COP: Hey, fellas, this old dame passed out in the street all of a sudden!

Ad libs of concern. Miriam brings a glass of water and hands it to the Cop. Sam and the Professor help the Lady into a chair. All gather round.

REVEREND *not looking at her*: Why, she's barely breathing!

COP: She might have broken her ankle or something. I'll get a cab to take her to the hospital.

PROFESSOR: Better move fast, it's rush hour.

Exit Cop. Dead silence for a second. Then Bill takes a step towards the Lady in Grey.

BILL: Fly?

FLY *coming to life*: God, what an ugly puss. What happened to you?

BILL: I tripped on a lump of dirt – Gorilla Baxley.

FLY: Gone?

BILL *indicating hat*: G-O-N.

FLY: Very interesting.

The gang has gathered around her, putting their weapons on the table. She goes up to Baby Face and pulls from his jacket a gun he has kept concealed.

FLY: How you doing, Baby Face?

BABY FACE: Aw, not bad.

FLY: Good boy. Things running smoothly, Governor?

GOVERNOR: Pretty well, thank you, boss.

FLY: All right, men. Item One: The bank job you've all been waiting for is scheduled for the day after tomorrow.

ALL: Christmas Eve!!

FLY: Ho ho ho.

GOVERNOR: Brilliant!

REVEREND: Which bank?

FLY: You'll find out. Item Two: Last week's car heist. Well, Bill? You were gone a long time. We were getting worried.

BILL: Thanks for your concern. I got the cars to Detroit, fresh coat of paint, unloaded them real easy. We cleared eight hundred bucks, it's waiting for you in the usual place. With receipts for my expenses.

FLY: Very good. Did you happen to run into Tessie Miller in Detroit?

Miriam breaks a glass. The gang snickers.

BILL: What if I did?

FLY: Well, it doesn't really matter. It's just that I saw Tessie today. She had a new silver fox-piece around her neck, Bill. She said it was a gift from a friend, Bill. She told me it cost three hundred dollars, Bill.

BILL: Three hundred clams. My, my.

FLY: Three hundred clams. My, my.

BILL: Don't you wish you had friends like that?

FLY *taking out a cigarette*: Could you give me a light, Bill? *Bill lights her cigarette. The gang stares in horror. As the match strikes, title on screen:* THE FATAL FLAME! *Freeze onstage breaks when the Fly exhales.*

FLY: Governor, you remember the matter we discussed earlier?

GOVERNOR *purring*: Certainly.

FLY: We'll go ahead with that plan. Item Three: You've rehearsed the Prinzmeyer Pharmacy job, right?

GOVERNOR: All set to go, boss.

FLY: Good. That seventy-five bucks a month means a lot to us.

BILL: More chicken feed.

FLY: You can sit this one out, Bill. For the rest of you, the Pharmacy's at the corner of Jackson and Fifteenth. Sam and Baby, the back door. Professor, lookout.

PROFESSOR: But I –

FLY: Don't interrupt! Governor, you and the Reverend take the front door. We're going to make a nice example of Mr. Prinzmeyer. All right, you can have your rods back. It's time for the Fly to buzz off.

SAM: Wait a minute, there's something else! Where am I going to unload that goddam church organ? I'm out three hundred fifty –

COP *offstage, getting closer:* 'That old Bilbao moon, la la la la . . .'

FLY *sotto voce*: You'll have to work that one out for yourself.

COP: I'm back. I finally got a cab. *The Fly faints in his arms.* She all right?

GOVERNOR *mock-puzzled*: Oh, she just seem to be coming round.

COP: Well, I better get her to a hospital.

He carries the Fly out. The others hold till they exit. All are uncomfortable in Bill's presence. Title on screen: A TICKLISH SITUATION!

BABY FACE: Bill, I just wanna say . . .

The Governor stops him. Pause. Dead silence.

BILL: Awright, lay off! What the hell is this, an old ladies' home?

BABY FACE: Bill, you don't understand.

BILL *roughing him up*: Don't tell me I don't understand, jocko. You think I don't know what's going on around here? You think I gotta read it in Braille? I ain't afraid to light no broad's cigarette, no matter what it means. And I can take you guys on one at a time or all together. So if any of you gimps wants to see your chapeaus up there on a nail behind Dr. Wakasaki – you can meet me in the back room! *Exit, glowering.*

REVEREND: Well, we all know what we have to do. But how, may I ask, are we going to do it?

BABY FACE: I dunno.

REVEREND: Of course not.

BABY FACE: Lay off!

PROFESSOR: There's gotta be a way out of this, lemme think . . .

SAM *sarcastic*: Maybe you'll think of some gadget, then when he touches it, he bumps himself off.

PROFESSOR: Say, you know, that's not a bad idea, lemme see . . .

GOVERNOR *quietly and authoritatively*: Gentlemen. *They all look up.*

GOVERNOR: Not to worry, Mr. Cracker will be put out of way without any help from us.
Ad lib confusion from the gang.

GOVERNOR: You recall minor job to be done this evening on unfortunate pharmacist?
Ad libs: 'Yeah, so what about it?'

GOVERNOR: When we perform such job, is usually no evidence. This evening, will be evidence. Gentlemen, I give you – and the police – *He display's Bill's gun, which he has palmed or pick-pocketed during the Fly's exit, wrapped in his silk handkerchief.* Mr. Cracker's revolver.
Gasps of astonishment from the gang.

REVEREND: A veritable genius!

BABY FACE: Hey, that ain't fair!

GOVERNOR *smiling*: Very perceptive, Baby Face. *He pokes Miriam who has buried her face in her hands with his cane.* Beer Miriam.
Tableau.

SWITCH FLOT

Lights dim on the saloon and come up on the street, where the Salvation Army – Mary, Jane, Hannibal, and Ben – marches on, led by Lillian Holiday. Title on screen: MEANWHILE, VIRTUE MOBILIZES.

LILLIAN *sings*:

Look all around you
Look all around you
Look all around you, a man is about to drown
A woman is screaming 'Help me,' a child is falling down.
Don't move another step!
Stop, stay right there!
People need help all around you –
Don't you even care?

Are you completely blind?
You've time to greet your brother, but none for all
    mankind!
Forget about your dinner
Have you forgotten, sinner
How many stand in line?
How many stand in line?
I know you'll say, 'The poor are always with us.'
'The world's unjust and that's how it will stay.'
Here's how we answer you: You've got to stand up
Forget your fears and fight with us today.
So bring on the tanks and the cannon
And squadrons of planes let there be
And battleships on the sea
Just to conquer one small bowl of soup for every poor
    man
Just to conquer one small bowl of soup for every poor
    man!

LILLIAN & ARMY *sing*:

Let every man come join us
Our mission to fulfil
The Army that is small but strong
Is made up of men of good will

LILLIAN:

Forward march, chin up, take weapons, prepare!
People need help all around you – so you've got to care!

Lights come up immediately on the bar, as the Army marches in.
LILLIAN: God's blessing on all here!
PROFESSOR: Sweet Jesus!
LILLIAN *distributing tracts*: It is never too late to think of
Jesus, brothers.

BABY FACE *grabbing her*: Do ya love your neighbour, sister?

LILLIAN: Stop that, brother. A man can't love his fellow humans until he loves the Lord. We will sing to stir your souls. Number five, 'March Ahead'. Brother Hannibal.

HANNIBAL *blows a pitch pipe.*

ARMY *sings*:

> March ahead to the fight
> Where Satan's pow'r is at its height
> Sing ye now, use your might
> Let your song ring through the night
> Soon you will see the morning light
> And with the morning Our Lord Jesus Christ
> Hallelujah!

PROFESSOR: Ya know, it's kind of catchy.

REVEREND *very exaggerated*: Oh, sister, you have moved me. I should like to repent.

SISTER MARY: A convert already!

LILLIAN: Sing with us, brother!
They repeat the hymn, the Reverend joining in.

PROFESSOR: About time we saw you praying, Reverend.
The gang laughs.

LILLIAN: Shame on you! This man wants to forsake his life of sin, and you just laugh!

REVEREND: Pay no attention to them, sister. Your singing does my heart good. I am a miserable sinner, but I feel comfort in the presence of a holy person such as yourself.
He is on his knees next to her, embracing her, etc.

LILLIAN *disentangling herself*: Brother . . .

BABY FACE: Oh, brother!

REVEREND: I feel I can confide in you, Sister – Sister – what is your name, Sister?

SAM: And what's your telephone number?

The gang laughs.

LILLIAN: I am Sister Lillian Holiday.

REVEREND *passionately*: Sister Lillian!

LILLIAN *trying to escape him*: And this is Sister Mary, and Sister Jane, Brother Ben Owens, and Brother Hannibal Jackson with the trombone.

PROFESSOR *aside to the Governor*: She's the one they call 'Hallelujah Lil' – the Saint of South Canal Street!

GOVERNOR: Most edifying.

BABY FACE: She's got some build on her for a saint!

The gang laughs. Lillian starts to rebuke them.

REVEREND: Don't mind them, Sister Lillian. Let me tell you my story. I was brought up without benefit of your divine guidance. My Ma, rest her soul, kept me alive by selling her body. And when she died, my dad sold it again, to the medical students. All for my sake!

MARY: Ugh!

REVEREND: It's true, Sister. And as a consequence, it was inevitable that my hands should of strayed onto other people's property for a rather large proportion of my life.

JANE: Not so, brother.

REVEREND: Not when the blessed Army is here to rescue me, Sister. For I deeply resent the error of my ways, now that I feel closer to you – and to God. My remorse is great.

PROFESSOR: Ain't it the truth?

The gang laughs.

REVEREND: But I want to make a clean breast of my sins. I want to donate all my ill-gotten gains to the cause.

Jane comes forward with a collection basket.

HANNIBAL *beaming*: We know the saying: There is more joy in Heaven –

REVEREND *dropping all piety*: Over *us* than there is over you, for sure – so *here's* my contribution. *Spits in basket and throws it back at Jane, who shrieks.*

LILLIAN: Shame on you, brother! I've had enough! I'm going to preach you a sermon!

PROFESSOR *to the Reverend*: Oh, boy! Now look what you got us in for!

During the sermon the gang razzes Lillian, reacts in exaggerated horror, tries to flirt with her, etc., gradually getting more menacing.

LILLIAN: The topic for today's sermon, brother, is the rat. Isaiah 66:17; 'The abomination and the rat, they shall come to an end together, saith the Lord.' Now, I think you all know what a rat is: It's a dirty little animal that lives in the worst part of town.

BABY FACE: Here we is, sweetheart.

LILLIAN: A rat is a troublemaker, brothers. A rat stinks of garbage the way a drunken man stinks of whiskey. A rat carries disease, as a hoodlum carries his gun and blackjack. *Wandering among them, she has come to the Governor and picked up his cane to gesture with. Now she pulls it apart, does a take when she sees blade inside, nervously hands it back.*

PROFESSOR: Easy there, Sister.

LILLIAN *regaining her energy*: He lives in the darkest, dirtiest holes he can find. He hides from the good people who live in the poor parts of town, the ones who only want to live right and walk decently with their Lord. Because that's not what a rat wants, brothers.

BABY FACE: And what does he want, dollface?

LILLIAN: He wants to live off those good people, creep out of his hole when they're not looking and steal the bread from their mouths. That's why decent people hate rats. And you . . . *Pause* . . . are rats.

SAM *quizzically*: Now I never looked at it in that light before. *At this point Bill enters unobtrusively from the back room. The gang has not taken Lillian's insult lightly, though they restrain their anger. Their behaviour starts to get less frivolous and more menacing.*

LILLIAN: But there's a way out for the rat, brothers.

BABY FACE *trying to grab her*: Yeah, what?

LILLIAN: The rat could reform –

REVEREND: Could he now?

LILLIAN: – clean himself up –

PROFESSOR: I'll bet.

LILLIAN: Come out of his hole and – and get a decent job, so to speak.

GOVERNOR: And be a decent churchmouse!

LILLIAN: Yes he could, brother, he could! But he doesn't!

SAM: Aw, too bad.

LILLIAN: And do you know why?

BABY FACE: No, why, beautiful?

LILLIAN: Because he's afraid! *They are surrounding her now: she resists panic.* Yes, brothers, a rat is a coward. It doesn't take courage to commit his crimes – just a shortage of policemen and a dark street. But he's afraid to come in out of the darkness, because he's got no faith. He thinks the whole world's made of rats like him, because a rat who knifes a good man in the back on Monday will knife his brother rat on Tuesday. So don't be a rat! Don't live in fear and darkness. Come into the light of Jesus and live decent! Because the rats will turn against you in the end, but Jesus is always with you!

BABY FACE *grabbing her*: I'm with you, baby!

The gang closes in on her. The Army tries to break through.

LILLIAN *inside the din*: Let go of me.

BILL *over all the hubbub*: GET YOUR MEAT HOOKS OFF HER! *Everyone quietens down.*

BABY FACE: Jesus, Bill, I'm sorry.

BILL: You get these Holy Rollers out of here, and fast.

HANNIBAL: Come along, Sisters. We've been wasting our time.

MIRIAM *suddenly running from behind the bar*: Oh, God, take me with you! Get me out of this awful place.

The Army looks at one another, astonished. The gang laughs.

BILL: Awright, you Benedict Arnold. Now get out of here, all of youse, before I throw you out.

HANNIBAL: Come, sisters.

LILLIAN: Well, I'm staying.

BILL: Oh, you are, are you

The Army, with Miriam, has reached the top of the stairs.

LILLIAN: Brother Hannibal, if I'm not back in two hours, bring help.

HANNIBAL *going*: God go with you, sister – and preserve me from the migraine I'm getting.

The Army goes. Ben, the last out, gives one last loud boom on his bass drum as he goes.

BILL: So you're staying.

LILLIAN: You may be the notorious Bill Cracker, but you don't frighten me.

BILL: Oh, don't I?

LILLIAN: King Nebuchadnezzar was a bigger crook than you, and he didn't frighten Daniel.

BILL: King who?

LILLIAN: King Nebuchadnezzar. He ruled his gang with an iron fist, but even he couldn't stand up to God. And when it was over, they threw him out and he had nothing but grass to eat.

PROFESSOR: Can we get you a plate of grass, Bill?

BILL: Shuddup! Hey, don't you guys have a job to do or something? Beat it while your shoes are good.

GOVERNOR *ironic smile*: Only too glad to oblige, Bill.

The gang piles out the back door. Baby Face, as he reaches door starts to tell Bill something.

BABY FACE: Hey, Bill, they want to –

GOVERNOR *cutting him off*: Not wise, Baby Face. *Baby Face leaves, upset. Governor takes one last look at Bill.* Goodnight, Miss Hallelujah Lillian. Goodbye, Mister William Cracker. *He leaves. Bill watches him go, takes a bottle of whiskey from the bar, pours two drinks, brings them over to a table.*

BILL: The bums! You have to sew your pockets shut to keep their hands out. Siddown!

Lillian sits, nervously.

BILL: Now tell me about this king who ate grass. What was his name?

The lights begin to fade, slowly.

LILLIAN: N-Nebuchadnezzar.

Fade out.

Title on mirror: WHEN THE ARMY OF THE LORD DOES BATTLE . . . CUPID OFTEN CALLS THE SHOTS. *When the lights come up again, it is late evening. There are several empty whiskey glasses on the table in front of Lillian.*

LILLIAN: You've got it all wrong. You've misjudged us, admit it. You've had the wrong idea of us all these years, just like that king had of Daniel, the one who ate grass, what was his name?

BILL: Nebuchadnezzar.

LILLIAN: Right. He repented of his ways, and joined the Salvation Army – and that's what you should do, too.

BILL: Maybe I should.

LILLIAN: You're wasting your life. You don't need murders and thefts and hard liquor to keep you happy. The Army is always happy. It's music and light and joy. That's why I came to work there, for the joy. I want to see people happy, and so does the Army.

BILL: You want 'em to be happy your way.

LILLIAN: I keep telling you, you've got us wrong. We're not afraid to see things your way. *Impulsively, she jumps up and gives him a quick kiss. They are both a little embarrassed by this.*

BILL: . . . All that drum beating and those songs about Jesus.

LILLIAN: We have songs that don't have anything to do with Jesus!

BILL: I can guess what they're like.

LILLIAN: I bet you can't! *Getting up shakily.* I need a hat for this. Have you got a sailor hat? *Going up to hatrack before he can answer, she puts on Gorilla Baxley's homburg.* Now this is a common song, about the life of common sailors. Listen. *Title on screen above*: THE SAILORS' TANGO. *Light dims to a very harsh white spot on Lillian. Bill watches raptly.*

LILLIAN *sings*:

Hey there, we're sailing off to Burma this evening
With enough good Scotch on board to float all the way
Plus a crate of great cigars: 'Henry Clay'
Had it up to here with girls, so we're leaving
'Cause it's time to start a brand new day
Yes, it's time to start a brand new day.

Now, we never ever smoke other brands of cigars
And this leaky tub will barely get us to Burma
And we don't need that God who's up there in the stars
And we don't need all his laws on terra firma
So all right, goodbye!
And the ship sails away, and it may reach Rangoon
And as for God, well, we don't get him
And it may be that God feels just the same about us
So let's hope he doesn't let it upset him
And all right, goodbye!

We're off on the sea and it's 'Who gives a damn?'
Life's perfect, 'cause nothing is missing
And your dreams of glory? Just take 'em and scram!
The whole world's our pot and – we're pissing!

Ah, the sea is blue, so blue
And all the world goes on its way
And when the day is over
We start another day
Ah, the sea is blue, so blue
And that's how it's gonna stay
Ah, the sea is blue, so blue
Ah, the sea is blue, so blue
Ah, the sea is blue, so blue
The sea is blue.

Hey there, we might go to a movie if you want to
They'll make us pay, we don't care, me and you
We won't grow our grey hairs, not until they're due
People like us are entitled to have a bit of fun, too
'Cause there's not a thing we have to do
No, there's not a thing we have to do.

Now, we never smoke cigars that cost less than five
  cents
And that cheap black bread gives us indigestion
And we don't give a damn what makes other guys
  tense
And as for soul-searching – there's just no question:
That's not why we're here!
And our life sails away, and who knows how it ends?
And as for God, well, let's forget him
And it may be that God feels just the same about us
So let's hope he won't let it upset him
Yeah, why should he care?

Our lives are our own and we don't give a damn
Life's perfect, 'cause nothing is missing
And your dreams of glory? Just take 'em and scram!
The whole world's our pot and – we're pissing!

Ah, the sea is blue, so blue
And all the world goes on its way
And when the day is over
We start another day
Ah, the sea is blue, so blue
And that's how it's gonna stay
Ah, the sea is blue, so blue
Ah, the sea is blue, so blue
Ah, the sea is blue, so blue
The sea is blue.

Spoken over the music:
Now all we need is for a storm to blow up!
Relax, there's the docks of Rangoon up ahead.
– Hey, wait, that's only a bank of black clouds in the air!
Jesus . . . and the waves are going crazy out there!
Jesus, in a minute the whole lot of us will be dead!

Sings again:
Well, we knew we'd have to die somewhere
Yeah, we knew we'd have to die somewhere

Down goes the ship and soon the sea washes over
Nothing but sharks down there to show a drowned
man the way
Scotch is no use to them or crates of 'Henry Clay'
Where they're going there are no girls who need a
lover
They won't ever see another day
They won't ever see another day

And the water comes up, and the ship's going down
And as for a harbour, we don't get one
Just a wreck of a ship and a glimpse of a shore
But of course, one can't let it upset one!

So all right, goodbye!
Then for once, you don't hear all that big talk in the
    air
And the big talkers suddenly look smaller
And they're down on their knees and mumbling
    about their Father who's up there
And they're starting to weigh the sins their souls must
    bear
And that's how they die.

And now let me tell you a fact that we all ought to
    know:
You may have been bragging a lifetime or so
But now, when it matters, you're shitting!

*The Army has come back just in time to hear Lillian say this.
Gasps, which she and Bill don't notice.*

Ah, the sea is blue, so blue
And all the world goes on its way
But when your day is over
There is no other day.
Ah, the sea is blue, so blue
You don't have that long to stay
Ah, the sea is blue, so blue
Ah, the sea is blue, so blue
Ah, the sea is blue, so blue
The sea is blue

HANNIBAL: Sister Lillian!
LILLIAN *exhausted, calm*: Oh. Brother.
HANNIBAL: What are you doing?
LILLIAN: I was preaching a sermon to this sinner.
HANNIBAL: A sermon? To one man? What was your text?

Take off that hat, you look ridiculous. And what's that on your breath? This is scandalous.

MARY: It really is shocking.

HANNIBAL: I'm reporting you to the Major. Shame, Lillian.

BILL *to Hannibal*: Leave her alone, creep.

HANNIBAL: And you keep out of this. You don't have your gang of roughnecks here to threaten us now. Come on, Lillian.

LILLIAN *sadly, to Bill*: I have to go eat my grass now.
The Cop enters.

COP: Are you Bill Cracker?

HANNIBAL: Certainly not!

BILL: I'm Cracker, Hawkshaw, what's your problem?
Lillian, feeling guilty, is hiding her head on Hannibal's shoulder.

COP *to Bill*: Where were you at seven o'clock this evening?

BILL: I was here.

COP: Any witnesses?

BILL *points to Lillian*: Her.

COP *suggestively*: Just her? *Bill nods. The Cop goes to Lillian.* Miss, were you and this man alone here at seven o'clock this evening?

LILLIAN: Seven o'clock?

COP: Just over an hour ago.

LILLIAN: Alone? Here? *She looks at Hannibal.* Well, I was here, and there were some others with us, and then – and then – we all left, and I just came back right now.

COP: I see. *Going back to Bill*: Cracker, you're under arrest for the murder of Jacob Prinzmeyer, pharmacist, at seven o'clock tonight. They found your gun at the scene.
Bill automatically goes for his gun, can't find it, looks to back room, looks at Lillian, who looks guiltily away. Projection: The Governor displaying Bill's revolver.

BILL: So that's it. You light her cigarette, and wham!

MARY: Smoking cigarettes too!

JANE: Really, Lillian!

Hannibal and the Army hustle Lillian up the stairs. At the door, Lillian stops to look back at Bill. He turns away and holds up his hands; the Cop snaps handcuffs on him. Tableau. Blackout. Title on screen above: INTERMISSION.

Switch + 1 off

Act Two

The Canal Street Mission. Chairs, benches, a podium, a banner. It all looks rather seedy. Upstairs, the tiny room Lillian, Jane and Mary share. Lillian's suitcase on an iron cot. As lights come up, the orchestra plays 'March Ahead', rousingly. Title on Screen: CANAL STREET MISSION — HARD TIMES FOR HALLELUJAH LIL! *Lights up to reveal Lillian and Major Stone (whom we have not seen before), facing each other.*

MAJOR: Consorting with hardened criminals. In a tavern. Singing disreputable songs. It's a serious matter, Lieutenant Holiday.

LILLIAN: Major —

MAJOR: This is not the sort of thing I need just now. I'm being asked to find a place for Sister Miriam, organize the Christmas celebration, keep the daily prayer meetings going, give a lecture at the Chamber of Commerce — and in the midst of all this, I'm told that my most devoted worker is creating scandal and ought to be dismissed. You have no right to do this to me, Lillian. Have you any way of explaining your conduct?

LILLIAN: Major, we have to approach men like these in their own world. We have to preach to them in their own language. That's all I was doing.

MAJOR *brightening*: I was hoping you'd be able to clarify this for me.

LILLIAN: Major, our Jesus consorted with publicans and sinners.

MAJOR: So He did, so He did. And all for the best. This

song you sang, it wasn't a profane song, was it? Just somewhat couched in the vernacular, I suspect.

LILLIAN: Well, yes, you could say that.

MAJOR: I'm sure it was all right. Brother Hannibal isn't used to such things, you know. He's a sensitive man, sensitive. Perhaps you'll sing me a bit of it, just to be safe. Would you mind, Sister Lillian?

LILLIAN: Not at all.

MAJOR: It's about sailors, I'm told.

LILLIAN: Yes, you see, they're drowning, and it goes like this. *Sings*:

> Then for once you don't hear all that big talk in the air
> And the big talkers suddenly look smaller
> And they're down on their knees and mumbling about
>   their Father who's up there
> And they're starting to weigh the sins their souls must
>   bear
> And that's how they die
> And now let me tell you a fact that we all ought to
>   know:
> When you stand before the throne where our Lord is
>   sitting
> You may have been bragging a lifetime or so
> But now, when it matters – you're worried!
>
> Ah, the sea is blue, so blue
> And all the world goes on its way . . .

She trails off. Spoken:

And that's the gist of it.

MAJOR: Yes, I see. Well, that's really quite a serious song, isn't it? The last rhyme is a bit weak, but otherwise it seems just fine. No, I don't see anything wrong in that.

LILLIAN: Then I can stay?

A knock at the door.

MAJOR: Excuse me a minute, Sister Lillian. *She goes to the door and admits the Cop.* What can we do for you, officer?

COP: I'm looking for Miss Holiday.

MAJOR: Yes, she's right here. *puzzled?*

COP: That statement you were going to write out for me, Miss.

LILLIAN: Yes, I have it right here. *Takes it from her uniform pocket and gives it to him.*

COP: Yes ... hm ... good ... wait. Miss Holiday: It says here that you *were* alone with the suspect between 6.30 and 7.30. Yesterday you told us you didn't arrive there till later. Now which is right?

LILLIAN: This is right, officer. I was alone with him for that hour.

MAJOR: Lieutenant Holiday!

COP: Then he has an alibi for that hour.

LILLIAN: He did not commit that crime, officer. When I talked to you yesterday, I didn't know what was at stake. *To Major*: I can't let my own reputation stand in the way of the truth.

MAJOR: You know what this means, Lieutenant.

COP: You're letting the toughest crook in Chicago slip through our hands, Miss.

LILLIAN: I'm telling you the truth, officer.

COP: That's not what the Commissioner needs just now. *Exit, disgruntled.*

MAJOR: You'd better go upstairs and pack, Lieutenant. And change out of your uniform. You're relieved of all duties. I'm sorry. Major Irving at the central office will give you your orders from now on.

LILLIAN: Major, I was struggling for that man's soul.

MAJOR: I realize that, Lieutenant. But the Devil was struggling for yours as well. And it's not up to me to say who won.

Lillian turns and goes up the stairs. Hannibal, Ben, Miriam, now in uniform, Mary and Jane have come in during this last exchange.

MAJOR: Sister Lillian has been relieved of her duties here. *To Mary and Jane*: You two sisters will help her pack and receive her final notes on the sermon for tonight's meeting. *Jane and Mary follow Lillian up the stairs.*

MAJOR: Sister Miriam, you'll be able to move your belongings out of the kitchen now. You'll have Miss Holiday's old room. Meantime, will you start preparing the soup for tonight?
Miriam, upset by Lillian's ouster, looks displeased.
Brother Owens can show you how.
Miriam brightens up.
Captain Jackson, you'd better help me clean the hall and pass out the hymn books. It's getting late.

HANNIBAL *taking a pile of hymnbooks*: I want to be careful about overwork, Major. I'm getting the old ache in my head again.

MAJOR: All right, everybody. Get to work.
Miriam and Ben exit to the kitchen.

JANE *half-singing, on her way up the stairs*: Ah, the sea is blue, so blue . . .

MARY: . . . And pride will have a fall.
They giggle.

LILLIAN *packing upstairs, while Jane and Mary whisper to each other*: Do you want to hear the sermon or don't you?

MARY: Well, I don't know if I can preach one of those modern vernacular sermons you deliver so well. I'm not as aware of the ins and outs of progressive ideas as you are.

HANNIBAL *just before reaching the bench*: Oh! Oh! My head!
Collapses, scattering hymnbooks all over.

MAJOR: Brother Hannibal! Miriam, get the smelling salts!
Miriam and Ben run out and help the Major rouse Hannibal.

LILLIAN: I was thinking we'd make the sermon on that subject exactly. We could use the image of a radio. Like this: Lots of people today think it's fashionable to laugh when God is mentioned, and say, 'Yes, but have you ever seen Him? You can't believe in something you can't see.' There's even a famous French astronomer who said, in print, 'I searched with my telescope from one end of the universe to the other, and I couldn't find God.'

JANE *writing in a tiny notebook*: '. . . . and you couldn't find God.'

HANNIBAL *waking up*: It started five years ago. Just before the Army took me in. I was – I was – well, I don't remember what I was, but I remember something hit me on the head, hard, and ever since then I black out occasionally.

MAJOR: How often?

HANNIBAL: Oh, not that often. *He immediately faints again.*

LILLIAN: Well, of course he couldn't find God. He was using the wrong instrument. You don't see God with a telescope. And here I thought we'd bring in the miracle of radio.

JANE: The radio?

LILLIAN *very fast*: It's like this: One day, suddenly, you're told that there are waves in the air that carry sound. And you can't see them. And you don't believe they exist. Then one day you set up a crystal set, and put on the earphones – and all at once you hear music! And *then*, you believe.

JANE *utterly confused*: The radio?

HANNIBAL: Where am I?

BEN: You had a fainting spell.

HANNIBAL: Fainting spell! It started five years ago, just before the Army –

MAJOR: Yes, Brother, we understand. Now why don't you go into the kitchen and relax for a while? Sister Miriam will fix you a Seidlitz powder.

Ben and Mirian walk Hannibal shakily into the kitchen. The Major sighs and starts to pass out hymnbooks. .

LILLIAN: God is always broadcasting. His music is always

on the air. It's just a question of using the right tool, the right part of you, to hear Him with. We can all see God in our hearts, and hear His music in our souls: it's just a matter of tuning in on His wave-length. *She has meanwhile packed her few belongings and picked up her suitcase.* Now, do you think you can follow all that?

MARY: Oh, yes, it seems quite simple.

JANE: I think my notes ought to help.

LILLIAN: I see the Mission is in good hands. *She comes downstairs.*

MAJOR: Well, Lillian, goodbye and good luck.

LILLIAN: Yes, I'm leaving now. I'm sure your Mission will keep the great work going, you've got some fine workers here. Mary's going to give a simply glowing sermon, aren't you, darling?

HANNIBAL *who has staggered to the kitchen door; weakly:* Lillian, I . . .

LILLIAN *turning at the street door:* You hypocritical . . . stool pigeon!

She runs out, almost crying. At the same time Sam pokes his head in.

SAM: Begging your pardon, would this be the Salvation Army?

JANE: I'm sorry sir. The meeting won't begin for a while. Could you come back later?

SAM *pushing right past her:* Oh, then this *is* the Salvation Army. I knew it, and you're the lovely ladies I heard singing yesterday. Don't you all have wonderful voices. And what a charming place. *Comes to the Major.* You must be the General. General, I want to tell you, it touches my heart when I think of the fine work your dedicated band is doing to spread a little joy in the world. That girl who makes the speeches – now isn't she an inspiration? Best thing I've heard since William Jennings Bryan. Magnificent!

MAJOR: I see, and you're one of the men from Bill's Beer Hall
are you? Well, you won't find her here any longer.

SAM: Are you equating me with that lot of numbskulls and
rapscallions? Field Marshal, you've done me an injury.
I'm here on *your* behalf, and you wound me to the quick.
I ought to walk right out that door. *Jane holds it open for
him. He starts to leave but zooms back.* But I can't return
hurt for hurt. I couldn't leave without telling you about
the joy I've come here to bring you.

MAJOR: Yes, just why have you come here?

SAM: Brigadier, have you ever rejoiced in an organ?

MAJOR: I beg your pardon?

SAM: I mean, have you ever thrilled to the sound of a great
cathedral organ?

MAJOR: Well –

SAM: Well, then you know how that passionate echoing
music stirs the crowds. As it happens, this is your lucky day,
Commander. I'm prepared to offer you a fabulous bargain
on an organ. It just came into my family through an
unusual set of coincidences, it's no use to me and I'm
willing to let you have it at cost: only four hundred
dollars. Now how does that strike you?
*He has pulled the Major over to one side. Meantime Jane has
opened the door and the fold is starting to wander in for the
meeting: Drunks, eccentric old ladies, a few pious farmers, a
hooker, a blind man, etc.*

MAJOR: My dear sir, we have no space for an organ here.
Look at this place.

SAM: Yes, look at this place.

MAJOR That's just what I said.

SAM: And that's what I'm saying to you, Admiral. It's
evident to my eye that you need a little zing in your business. Don't forget the words of Henry Ford, that great
man.

MAJOR: What did he say?

SAM: You don't know what he said?

MAJOR: No, what did he say?

SAM: He said: 'I consider every offer'. Now Commodore, can
   you afford to ignore the sound advice of a prominent
   American?

MAJOR: I really have no time to deal with this –

SAM: It has the tone of a thousand angels!

MAJOR: We're about to start our meeting –

SAM: It's a purchase you'll never regret, I promise you!

MAJOR: All right.

SAM: You'll take it?

MAJOR: Yes – no! I'll speak to you afterwards.

SAM *sitting down*: Major, you've got a heart of gold.
   The Major goes to the pulpit.

MAJOR: Welcome, dear friends in Jesus. We will open our
   meeting tonight with Number Three in your hymnbooks,
   'Brother, Give Yourself a Shove.'

JANE: Rise, please.

ARMY *and fold sing*:

   Brother, give yourself a shove
   Let yourself not waver
   If you love the Lord above
   If you love the Lord above
   He will keep you in His favour
   Brother, give yourself a shove
   Brother, give yourself a shove
   Brother, give yourself a shove.

MAJOR: Be seated.
   *All sit, except the Army officers, who stand on either side of
   the Major on the podium. The Major opens the Bible and reads.*

MAJOR: Psalm 69. 'Save me, O God, for the waters are come
   in unto my soul. I sink in deep mire, where there is no
   standing . . .'

While the Major reads, lights fade on the Mission. Title on screen: MEANWHILE, IN THE ENEMY CAMP ... *Lights slowly come up on the Beer Hall, where Baby Face and the Governor are sitting at the bar – a few stools and a bit of rail will suggest the scene.*

BABY FACE *very jumpy*: Gimme one good reason!

GOVERNOR: Calm, Baby. Have drink. Whiskey heal all wound.

BABY FACE: I wanna know why we framed Bill. He was my only friend in the gang.

GOVERNOR: You are so young. But unless you get smarter, you not live to get much older.

BABY FACE: You better give me a straight answer – or you're gonna end up under Lake Michigan, in a cement kimono!

GOVERNOR: Did you know, Baby, Fly is long time planning merger with Gorilla Baxley gang?

BABY FACE: Wha? Jeez, I didn't know that.

GOVERNOR: When Bill rub out Gorilla, is A-number-One interference.

BABY FACE: But I thought Gorilla Baxley was our competition –

GOVERNOR: No, Gorilla was friend. Bill was big headache.

BABY FACE: But Bill was great! Bill was the toughest guy in the gang!

GOVERNOR: That is why he was big headache.

BABY FACE *jumping up, waving his gun*: You're confusin' me! And when I get confused, I start shootin'!

GOVERNOR: Not good to wave gat. Might hit valuable friend. *He karate-chops Baby Face's wrist and snatches his gun.* Permit me to offer piece of ancient oriental wisdom. *The Governor sings* SONG OF THE BIG SHOT. *As he sings, he methodically roughs Baby Face up, feinting and outmanoeuvring him at every turn, in rhythm. Sings:*

If you want to be a big shot
Start by learning to be tough
'Cause you'll never hit the jackpot
Till you like the going rough

All the little shots below you
Can be blown away like fluff
If they realize when they know you
That you won't take all their guff

Just don't get soft, baby
For God's sake never get soft, baby
Just keep on pounding him right where it hurts the
    most
And if a little shot's big noise should cause a bother
Don't let if get you down, I mean you're not his
    father

Just don't get soft, baby
For God's sake never get soft, baby.
No ifs or buts
Go on and kick him in the guts
Go on and kick him in the guts

Blackout on Beer Hall. Title on Screen: A SORTIE INTO
UNKNOWN TERRITORY. *Lights up on the Mission.*

MAJOR *finishing Psalm*: '. . . for the Lord heareth the poor,
and despiseth not His prisoners'.

EVERYONE: Amen.

Bill comes into the Mission. The Army, fold and Sam react.

MAJOR: And now, Sister Jane Grant will lead us in Number
Eight, 'Don't Be Afraid'.

*Jane comes up to the pulpit, evidently rendered quite nervous by
Bill's presence. During her song he sees Sam at the back of the
room and goes to him – as quietly as he can, but nonetheless*

attracting a great deal of attention. He is smoking a cigarillo, for which Ben officiously holds out an ashtray.

JANE *sings*:

> Don't be afraid
> Don't be afraid
> Though corruption leads you astray
> God will take you in His right hand
> He will show you the virtuous way
> Don't be afraid
> Don't be afraid
> Don't be afraid

The fold takes up the tune and hums it as Bill reaches Sam, who is very edgy. They converse in whispers.

SAM: Hello, Bill.

BILL: Where is she?

SAM: Where is who?

BILL: That broad who gives the sermons. I gotta see her.

SAM: Oh . . . I dunno . . . I don't think she's here.

BILL *louder, just as the fold finishes*: What do you mean, she's not here?

MAJOR *glaring at this source of noise*: That was lovely, Jane. And now – *Coldly* – *if* the congregation will give us their full attention, Captain Jackson will lead us all in the popular hymn, 'In our Childhood's Bright Endeavour', accompanied by chimes.

BILL: Where is he?

SAM *frantic*: How do I know?

MAJOR: Are you distressed, brothers? Can we be of some help to you?

SAM *seizing his chance*: I really must be going, Major – pressing business – thank you for everything – you've changed my life – goodbye – bless you – *Exit quickly, tripping over the podium.*

MAJOR *to Bill*: And you, brother? Can we be of help to you?

BILL: I don't know.

MAJOR: Perhaps you'll stay and pray with us?

BILL: I might stick around, at that.

MAJOR: Very good. *Going back to the pulpit.* Brother Jackson, if you will oblige.

HANNIBAL *sings*:

> In our childhood's bright endeavour
> We were warmed in mother's arms
> Now that warmth is gone forever
> Like our childhood's fading charms.

MARY *whispering*: Major, that's the man they found with Sister Lillian!

MAJOR *her face clouding over*: I see.

HANNIBAL *after clearing his throat to quiet them*:

> But the sound of church bells tolling
> Through our pain and our dismay
> So inspiring, so consoling –
> They are tolling still today

Lights down on the Mission, up on the Beer Hall. Lillian enters.

LILLIAN: Excuse me – where's Mr. Cracker?

GOVERNOR *smiling*: Mr. Cracker out to lunch. For about twenty year.

LILLIAN: Oh, that's not true.

BABY FACE: Girlie, wasn't you here when they took him away?

LILLIAN: Yes.

BABY FACE: So there must be something wrong with your head. He's in jail. Where did you think they was taking him, the Palmer House?

LILLIAN: But they let him out. He's free.

Baby Face and the Governor look at each other in consternation.

LILLIAN: I told them the truth, that he was here with me when that man was killed. So I'll just wait . . .

GOVERNOR: Not wise, Miss Holiday Lil.

Sam runs in, breathless.

SAM: They let him out! He's free! He's on the loose!

LILLIAN: Where is he?

SAM: The Salvation Army, Canal Street.

Lillian starts to run out; Baby Face grabs her.

BABY FACE: Hold on, Sister Salvation, you ain't going noplace.

GOVERNOR: You watch her, Baby Face. I take care of Mr. Cracker.

Exit the Governor, gun drawn. Sam swigs from his flask.

Lights down on the Beer Hall and up on the Mission.

MAJOR: And now, dear friends, our own Lieutenant Mary Pritchard will preach to you on the topic, 'God Is on the Air Waves'.

MARY: Thank you, Major. You know, ladies and gentlemen, a lot of people think you can't see God. *Long pause.* Well, and of course you can't. You don't see God, you hear Him. No, that's not what I mean . . . *Pause. Jane is miming 'telescope'.* Oh, yes, telescope! Thank you, Jane. Yes, people think you can't see God. A famous French astronomer actually wrote a letter to his telescope – I mean, he wrote a letter to a newspaper and said, 'I took my telescope, and I sort of poked around the whole world, but I couldn't see God'. Well, of course not. *Pause.*

A VOICE IN THE CONGREGATION: Where's Lillian?

MARY: You don't see God just because you have a telescope. It's not the right tool. But you can see Him if the right tool comes to hand.

Snickers in the audience.

I mean, what you need is a radio. I mean, God isn't on the radio, but –

MORE VOICES *stamping feet, pounding, hooting, etc*: We want Lillian! Where's Lillian! Where's the Hallelujah girl!

MARY *desperately shouting over the clamour*: – but if you use your ears, you can see Him! I mean, for Christ's sake, He broadcasts every hour!

A LOT OF VOICES: Lillian! Lillian! We want Lillian!

BILL *jumping up*: Yeah. Let's have Lillian Holiday! I got something to say to her. Where's she hiding?

MAJOR *topping all the clamour, sternly*: We won't be going on with this service until we have silence. *They quieten down.* Thank you for your brave effort, Sister Mary. *Mary retires from the podium, biting her lip.* This is the House of the Lord, brothers and sisters. Aren't you ashamed to confront Him with such behaviour? Now, as Miss Holiday won't be with us this evening –

BILL: Why won't she?

MAJOR: Miss Holiday has been dismissed from our service, Mr. Cracker. And you of all people should know the reasons. Now, as she won't be here, we'll continue our meeting with –

BILL *starting for the Major*: Why, you cheesy crumbbun – *He is about to grab the Major when the Governor comes in, gun drawn.*

GOVERNOR: Excuse me! I hope I am not interrupting. No one move, please.
Hannibal drops to the floor in a faint. Jane goes to revive him.

GOVERNOR: Just go on with your service. I see Mr. Cracker have been causing more trouble, but not to worry. He will soon be out of your way.
Dead silence.
Please to continue, Major.

MAJOR: – that beloved temperance ballad, 'The Liquor Dealer's Dream'.

GOVERNOR: One of my favourites!

MAJOR: Captain Jackson?

Title on screen: THE LIQUOR DEALER'S DREAM. *Hannibal, who has risen shakily to his feet, moves towards the podium, tries to change his mind and go back, is brought down to the podium again. Meantime, Bill, hands high, has made his way over to the Governor's side in response to the Governor's waves of his gun.*

HANNIBAL *sings*:

> At the bar, behind a pile of glasses
> Bleary-eyed, with puffy purple lips
> Sleeps a pale and sweaty liquor dealer
> Trousers bulging on his flabby hips
> And he dreams that he's gone to Heaven
> And he's called to the judgment board
> And he slugs down scotch in a frenzy
> Till he's drunker than a lord

ALL – *the Governor conducts with his gun*:

> Throw out the lifeline! Soul overboard!
> Throw out the lifeline! Soul overboard!

The Governor moves over to harmonize with Hannibal, who gets more frantic with each note. In the Governor's enjoyment of the song, he occasionally points his pistol at Hannibal's head instead of Bill's.

HANNIBAL *and the* GOVERNOR:

> And his knocking knees give way beneath him
> And he sees no help: he's doomed to fail
> And he feels the sword above his neckbone

And his shirt, that's damp from top to tail
And he shames himself in terror
There before all the heavenly host
And he thinks, 'Because I sell spirits
God had given up my ghost'.

ALL:

Throw out the lifeline! Soul overboard!
Throw out the lifeline! Soul overboard!

Hannibal has fainted at the end of the second verse; all sing the chorus while staring at him. The Governor picks out Jane, who is kneeling over him, and with his revolver motions her to get up and sing. During her verse, he waves goodbye jauntily and marches Bill out the front door at gunpoint.

JANE:

Then he wakes: his bleary eyes are staring
And the purple's paler on his lips
And he says, 'I've got to mend my ways now.'
Hikes his pants up on his flabby hips,
'And to widows and orphan children
To the needy, the old, the poor,
I will donate this dirty money
That has made my soul impure'.

The Governor and Bill disappear. Sounds of a scuffle. Gunshot. Splash. Everyone quails while singing.

ALL:

Soul safely rescued!
Soul safely rescued!

Bill comes back in with the gun. Everyone gasps.

BILL: Don't mind me, I'm just passing through – out the back window. I hope you'll be so good as to sing that last chorus again whilst I takes my leave. Just act natural. *He points the gun at the Army. While the group sings, he crosses the room, climbs the stairs, and out through the upstairs window.*

ALL:

   Soul safely rescued!
   Soul safely rescued!

LILLIAN *appearing at the front door just in time to see Bill disappear out through the window*: Bill!
   Everyone whirls around and gapes at Lillian. Tableau. Blackout.

Act Three

I

+ . l . on

Bill's Beer Hall. Orchestra plays BILBAO SONG. *Title on screen:*
CHRISTMAS EVE!

*As the lights come up, the gang, minus Sam and the Governor, is
assembled in the Beer Hall preparing for the robbery. Bill is
pacing; the others are watching the Professor work on an extravagant
machine, on one of the tables, that resembles a cross between a tele-
graph and a radio, with a large gramophone horn on top. Music out.*

REVEREND: What are you doing there, inventing the wheel?
PROFESSOR: Go peddle your snake oil!
BILL: Come on, Marconi, shake a leg.
PROFESSOR: Leave me be, willya? I gotta get the carbon
    diode hooked up to the generator.
BABY FACE: Yeah, he's gotta get the carbon diode hooked
    up to the –
BILL: Button it!
PROFESSOR: What a thing to leave to the last minute! If the
    Governor was here we'da' been organized.
BABY FACE: Yeah, if the Governor was here we'd – *Bill
    starts to move towards him.* – we'd – we'd haveta split the
    take six ways instead of five.
    Sam flounces on, grotesquely dressed as a woman.
SAM: Reverend! You forgot to get me the goddam hairpins!
GANG *ad lib whistles, exclamations, etc*: Oh, Mammy!
PROFESSOR: Well, aren't you the monkey's instep!

SAM: You like it, huh, boys? Of course, I don't know if I like it – an artist is never satisfied! Tell me, Baby Face, will it make the coppers think I'm your dear old mother?

BABY FACE: Gee, I dunno. My mother was a blonde.

REVEREND: And we can all testify to that!

General uproar. Sam wiggles gleefully.

BILL: Shake that moneymaker, sweetheart. Gentleman, Bill's Beer and Music Hall proudly presents the Queen of the Loop – Mammy Wurlitzer!

SAM *high tragedy*: Like that old dame says in the play: 'You can do whatever you like to me – but I'll still be Mother Goddam!'

Title on screen: THE MANDALAY SONG.

SAM *sings*:

> Mother Goddam's dive in Mandalay
> Seven rotten boards out on the bay
> Goddam, go tell that girl to get her ass in gear
> There's fifteen guys already lined up along the pier
> Watches in their hands and shouting 'Hey!'
> Is there just one girl in Mandalay?'
>
> All the girls are cute as they can be
> Even if they won't put out for free!
> Life would be so simple
> Everything in order
> If the guy who's in there
> Wasn't so damn slow
> Take your forty-five and shoot the door down
> Tell that guy in there he's holding up the show
> Faster Johnny, hey
> Faster Johnny, hey
> Sing the Song of Mandalay

ALL *sing*:

> Love doesn't have days and weeks to be reckoned
> Johnny, come on, don't you dare waste a second
> Will the moon shine every night over you, Mandalay?
> Will the moon shine every night over you?

SAM:

> Mother Goddam's dive in Mandalay
> Now it's rotting underneath the bay
> Goddam, that girl in there can rest her little rear
> There's not a single client out waiting on the pier
> No more watches left, no shouts of, 'Hey!'
> Not a single soul in Mandalay . . .
>
> Once the girls were cute as they could be
> Now there's not a one that's worth her fee!
> Life's no longer simple
> Nothing is in order
> There's no place like Goddam's
> All of them are gone.
> No more forty-fives to shoot the door down
> Where there's no one – the show just can't go on.
> Faster Johnny, hey
> Faster Johnny, hey
> Sing the man the Song of Mandalay

ALL:

> Love doesn't have days and weeks to be reckoned
> Johnny, come on, don't you dare waste a second
> Will the moon shine every night over you, Mandalay?
> Will the moon shine every night over you?

Uproarious laughter and hi-jinks. Suddenly the Professor's machine gives a small explosion, then starts to sputter and spark.

VOICE OF THE FLY *out of the gramophone horn*: Hello. Hello. The Fly is on the wing.

PROFESSOR: We got it! It's working! *They all gather round the machine.* Johnny, c'mere and help me with this. *Baby Face comes closer.* Turn this wheel. Very slowly. Now, when I get these two wires together . . . Slowly, slowly . . . Ow! Wait, stop! Stop! *Pulls his finger out of the wiring.* Oo, you really gave me a shock. All right, try it again.

Baby Face turns the wheel. The machine begins to give off static.

SAM: Fantastic!

FLY'S VOICE: All right, boys! Here are the assignments for tonight's caper: The place is the Manufacturer's National Bank. *Ad libs of delight from the gang.* Thought you'd like that. Professor. *Professor starts to say something.* Don't interrupt! At 10:15 you'll park the car on Division Street, out around the alley to the back entrance, and kill the alarm system. Mammy and Baby Face, mother and son as usual. Mammy covers the front entrance. Baby slips in the back way and knocks out the night-watchman.

SAM: You got that, Baby Face?

FLY'S VOICE: Don't ask stupid questions, you'll confuse him. Reverend will come down Clark Street, reconnoitre with Mammy at 10:23, and get the acetylene torch from him.

BILL: And be on time, dimwit.

FLY'S VOICE: Butt out, Bill. We don't need a repetition of yesterday's incident. Remember, you're still on probation. Now then: Sam will bring the car around to the alleyway. The rest of you yo-yos will meet him there at 10:35. Meantime Bill comes up the alley from the other side, picks up the bundle, and goes off in the opposite direction. And you better make good, Bill. Remember, if we can do without the Governor, we can do without you . . .

This last sentence comes out a bit distorted, as Baby Face, in his nervousness for Bill, turns the wheel more and more slowly. Bill makes a derisive gesture at the machine.

FLY'S VOICE: I saw that!

Everyone does a take.

FLY'S VOICE: All right, I'll meet you clowns back here at eleven. Synchronize watches. The time now is 9:14. *Electronic beep. They all start to head out.* Hold it, jerks! *They all stop dead.* Your alibis are in that bottle on the bar. Ten seconds to learn them. Oh, and boys – Merry Christmas. *Ad libs of 'Merry Christmas' back.* This is the Fly buzzing off!

Static. The machine goes dead. Bill finds the alibi slips, passes them out.

PROFESSOR *reading*: 'Ten till midnight, Hinky Dink Saloon. Witnesses: Tessie Miller, Eddie the Bartender.' Aw, not Tessie Miller.

Bill gives him a dirty look. He shuts up.

SAM: 'Cab ride to Forest Park, Yellow Cab number 35259. Witness: Cab driver, Steve Lardner, 111 North Clark.' What was I doing in Forest Park? Oh, well.

BABY FACE *and the* REVEREND *overlapping Sam's last line*: 'Birthday party at Captain Wolf's. Intimate dinner – *they realize their slips are identical* – with relatives. All evening. Sixty East Oak Street. Witnesses: Wolf family.

BILL *who has looked at his, nodded, and declined to read it aloud*: Have we got 'em? *All ad lib agreement.* Get rid of 'em.

All eat alibi slips, the Reverend spitting his.

PROFESSOR *swallowing*: Ugh.

BILL: Okay, now beat it while your shoes are still good. *The gang, impressed by his commanding manner, packs up quickly.*

SAM: Looks like Bill's right back in charge.

BABY FACE: Yeah, we was really worried about you. I thought you was gonna turn this place into another Holy Army mission.

Bill glares at them. Behind his back, the machine suddenly explodes. He whirls, gun drawn, sees what it is, puts his gun away.

REVEREND *begins to sing, softly*: 'Oh, holy night, the stars is brightly shining . . .'

The gang takes it up, laughing, as they run up the stairs.

BILL *over this*: All right, out, out, all of youse!

Lights dim. Bill pours himself a drink and sits morosely, his back to the door. Title on mirror: THE DESPAIR OF A LONELY CRIMINAL . . .

BILL: Goddam it.

Second title on mirror: . . . IS MATCHED BY THE SORROW OF A DOWNCAST SAINT. *Lillian enters, carrying her suitcase. Bill does not turn around.*

BILL: We're closed.

She comes down the steps.

BILL: I said we're closed. *He turns around.* Oh . . . it's you.

LILLIAN: I've left the Army, and I have no place to go in the meantime. So I thought I'd just see how you were getting along.

BILL: Well, that's real nice of you, but I'm busy. And you can't stay here, so you better go.

LILLIAN *seating herself at the bar*: You're not busy, Mr. Cracker. And I'm not going.

BILL: How do you know I'm not busy, Miss Holiday? What do you know about my life?

LILLIAN: I've seen it. I've seen through it. I saw what you did to that poor Japanese man yesterday.

BILL: Yeah, and did you see what he was gonna do to me? I just did it to him first, that's all.

LILLIAN: I didn't set you free so you could do that.

BILL: Set me free? Listen, where the hell do you get off, thinkin' you can make the world so much better that it is? I coulda hired a dozen broads to tell the cops what you told them.

LILLIAN: They wouldn't have been telling the truth.

BILL: The truth? Who cares about the truth? Since when do you carry keys to the pokey?

LILLIAN: They had you up for murder – and they let you out because they trusted me.

BILL: And when I got out I killed a guy. See, you had me all wrong.

LILLIAN: Aren't you even sorry?

BILL: Sorry? Yeah – I'm sorry I didn't get his hat for my collection.

LILLIAN: Is that all?

BILL: All? Oh, wait a minute. You mean, am I sorry you lost your job? Well, listen, sister, it ain't my fault, if Jesus fired you cause he's got a dirty mind.

LILLIAN: Jesus didn't fire me. Jesus is still with me.

BILL: Great, then what're you bothering me for? Why don't you go home and keep Him happy?

LILLIAN: I'm not worried about His happiness. I'm worried about yours.

BILL: I'm happy! I'm as happy as I can be! Open your eyes, why don't you? Take a look around you! Do you know where you are?

LILLIAN: Bill's Beer Hall.

BILL: Bill's Beer Hall, and I'm Bill. I run this place. I make good money out of what goes on here, which is none of your damn business so we won't talk about it – and you know what happens when I go outside?

LILLIAN: No.

BILL: Every man, woman, and child in the 43rd Ward says, 'There goes Bill Cracker,' and they touches their hats to me.

LILLIAN: They're afraid of you.

BILL: Yeah. And that makes me feel just great. I'm on my own. I got everything I want. And nobody ever gets in my way. P.S.: I can have any broad in Chicago. So what have I got to be unhappy about?

LILLIAN: I don't know. Why are you unhappy?

BILL: I ain't! And I don't need an unemployed hallelujah tootsie telling me how to run my life.

LILLIAN: You think that's all there is to me.

BILL: I don't see nothin' else.

LILLIAN: You don't think a woman can suffer like a man.

BILL: I don't care if she does.

LILLIAN: You do care. But you want to believe you don't care.

BILL: Try me.

LILLIAN: I'll make you care. I've got a song I want you to hear.

BILL: Can I get you a hat?

LILLIAN: I don't need one.

Title on screen: SURABAYA JOHNNY. *Lillian sings*

> I had just turned sixteen that winter
> When you came up from Burma to stay
> And you told me I ought to travel with you
> You were sure it would be okay
> When I asked how you made your living
> I can still hear what you said to me:
> You had some kind of job with the railway
> And had nothing to do with the sea
>
> You said a lot, Johnny
> All one big lie, Johnny
> You cheated me blind, Johnny
> From the minute we met
> I hate you so, Johnny
> When you stand there grinning, Johnny
> Take that damn pipe out of your mouth, you rat!
>
> Surabaya Johnny, no one's meaner than you
> Surabaya Johnny, my God, and I still love you so!

Surabaya Johnny, why'm I feeling so blue?
You have no heart, Johnny, and I still love you so!

At the start every day was Sunday
Till we went on our way one fine night
And before two more weeks were over
You thought nothing I did was right
So we trekked up and down through the punjab
From the source of the river to the sea:
When I look at my face in the mirror
There's an old woman staring back at me.

You didn't want love, Johnny
You wanted cash, Johnny
But I saw your lips, Johnny
And that was that.
You wanted it all, Johnny
I gave you more, Johnny
Take that damn pipe out of your mouth, you rat.

Surabaya Johnny, no one's meaner than you
Surabaya Johnny, my God, and I still love you so!
Surabaya Johnny, why'm I feeling so blue?
You have no heart, Johnny, and I still love you so!

Though your name should have told me different
I had hoped we would soon settle down
But in every saloon on the coastline
They would cheer when you came to town
And one day in a two-bit flophouse
I'll wake up to the roar of the sea
And you'll leave without one word of warning
On the ship waiting down at the quay

You have no heart, Johnny
You're just a louse, Johnny

How can you go, Johnny
And leave me flat?
You're still my love, Johnny
Like the day we met, Johnny
Take that damn pipe out of your mouth, you rat.

Surabaya Johnny, no one's meaner than you
Surabaya Johnny, my God, and I still love you so!
Surabaya Johnny, why'm I feeling so blue?
You have no heart, Johnny, and I still love you so!

Bill is crying. Neither he nor Lillian notices that during the song the Fly, disguised as a newsboy, has come in quietly through the back door.

LILLIAN: You see, Bill, you do care.

BILL: Like hell I do! And even if I do, so what! *He sings:*

If you want to be a big shot
Start by learning to be tough
'Cause you'll never hit the jackpot
Till you like the going rough
All the little shots below you
Can be blown away like fluff
If they realize when they know you
That you won't take all their guff

Just don't get soft, baby
For God's sake never get soft, baby
Just keep on pounding them right where it hurts the
    most
Because a big shot lives without all those emotions
So you can't knock him down with sentimental notions
Just don't get soft, baby
For God's sake never get soft, baby
No ifs or buts

>Go on and kick him in the guts
>Go on and kick him in the guts

Bill, drained, wheels away from Lillian, and sees the Fly.

FLY: Got a light?

BILL: Fly! Ten-thirty!

LILLIAN: What's wrong? Who's this boy?

BILL: Eleven o'clock! It's all over, isn't it?

FLY: It sure is.

LILLIAN: Bill, what's he saying?

FLY: I want a light for my cigarette.

BILL *striking a match*: Sure, sure, yes, a light. *The match won't ignite.* Light your own damn cigarette! *Gets up abruptly and runs out.*

LILLIAN: Bill!

FLY: And you can take your cheap suitcase and get out of here.

LILLIAN: Yes, I'm going. This is no place for me. I'm going back to the Salvation Army. Maybe they'll let me start at the bottom and work my way up again. They wouldn't dare throw me out: it's Christmas. I wish I knew what I've done.

Exit Lillian. The Fly has changed back into female costume. She turns out the lights and waits in the dark.

Orchestra plays THE MANDALAY SONG, *while on the screen is shown a film sequence, or a rapid sequence of slides showing the gang performing all the steps in the robbery, as described in the Fly's instructions. The last two shots show the money, waiting untended in the alley, and the gang, piled into their car and heading back to the Beer Hall, all smiles. As the music ends they burst in, turn on the lights.*

SAM: Boy oh boy oh boy! Fifty grand!

BABY FACE: Bill! Hey, Bill!

PROFESSOR: I'm gonna get me a lab that makes Menlo Park look like a phone booth!

REVEREND: Well, where is he?

BABY FACE: Bill!

SAM *to the Professor, as the other two hunt for Bill*: I'm gonna buy a yacht as big as a cathedral!

PROFESSOR: And instal your organ on it.

SAM: Right!

BABY FACE *in the back room*: Bill!

PROFESSOR: Every fish in the lake will go deaf.

Sam takes a playful swipe at the Professor: Baby Face interrupts them.

BABY FACE: Hey, Bill ain't here!

REVEREND: It seems our pie in the sky has flown the coop.

SAM: But didn't you see him out there?

PROFESSOR: No, there was nobody in the alley but a goddam newsboy.

SAM: But our fifty grand!

REVEREND: We'll never see a penny of it now!

FLY *rising from behind the bar*: Guess again. It's right here.

ALL: Fly!

PROFESSOR: You was the newsboy!

FLY: Damn straight.

SAM *going for the money*: Fifty grand! Come on Mammy!

The others elbow in for their share of the money; the Fly pushes them off.

FLY: Hold it! There's a little job to be done before we divvy up the boodle.

REVEREND: What kind of job?

FLY: Mr. Bill Cracker.

PROFESSOR: That's right. Why didn't he show?

FLY: Mr. Cracker was preoccupied with affairs of the heart. So he let our fifty grand slip his mind while a Salvation Army lassie sang him an anthem or two.

SAM: I don't believe it.

FLY: I saw it.

SAM: I believe it.

FLY: So I asked him for a light. *All react.* And this time I meant it. He knows all our plans and he's gone soft in the head over his religious sweetie. He may be in some little booth right now, telling some mackerel snapper all about us. And it's only one step from the confessional to the phone booth.

BABY FACE: Hey, we're in trouble.

FLY: Kee-rect, genius. Unless we shut his mouth before he opens it.

BABY FACE: Wow, when I think of Bill selling out – I just want to roll over and die.

FLY: Easy, Buster Brown. Don't start singing the blues just yet. There's no electric cord plugged into your chair.
Sam has surreptitiously started fondling the money.

FLY: And you keep your paws off! Nobody gets a cent of that till Bill is out of the way!

REVEREND: The money means nothing! Either we get him tonight or we have a one-way ticket to Hell tomorrow.

FLY: Just take care of business tonight. Tomorrow can take care of itself. Tomorrow, hmmph!

Lights change. Title on screen: BALLAD OF THE LILY OF HELL. *Projections of houseflies, enormously magnified, seen as if through red flames. The Fly sings:*

> You guys may not be inclined to worry if I burn in Hell
> If a chicken soaked in wine will cook to medium or well
> If a chicken soaked in wine will cook to medium or well
> You guys may not be inclined to worry if I burn in Hell
> Get this straight:
>
> That's a problem for tomorrow
> I don't need to borrow sorrow
> T'morrow's nothing, to be blunt
> You can shove it where you want!

Tips for tomorrow never pay
Tomorrow you'll regret what you did today
And soon enough you'll burn for it as well . . .
So who gives a hoot in hell?

– shove tomorrow where you want!

Now I bet you guys are thinking I want you to be concerned
Catch me when you see me sinking, save me so I don't
get burned
Catch me when you see me sinking, save me so I don't
get burned
Yeah, I bet you guys are thinking I want you to be
concerned
Get this straight:

I'll take care of that tomorrow
You don't need to borrow sorrow
T'morrow's nothing, to be blunt
You can shove it where you want

Tips on tomorrow never pay
Tomorrow you'll regret what you did today
And soon enough you'll burn for it as well
So who gives a hoot in Hell?

– shove tomorrow where you want!

BABY FACE *after the song*: Don't worry, Fly, we'll get him for
you.
FLY: Thanks, boys. I don't know what this gang's coming
too . . .
*The gang starts to leave up steps but slows down to listen as she
soliloquizes on.*

FLY: The Governor gone and Bill pulling these crazy stunts behind my back. You boys are all I've got. I don't want to see this operation fall apart . . . the gang's meant everything to me since my man disappeared five years ago . . . What am I getting so sentimental about! If I'm not careful *I'll* be the next one into the church! *She sees them clustered on the steps.* Cut the stalling! Get out of here and find that sacred-heart bastard!

They hurry out. Lights dim to a spot on her and she looks straight out at the audience, and sings:

When they count my sins in Heaven, then I'll get to
    know my luck
Is it furnace number seven or a harp for me to pluck?
Is it furnace number seven or a harp for me to pluck?
When they count my sins in heaven, then I'll get to
    know my luck
Got that straight?

Like I said, I'll know tomorrow
I don't need to borrow sorrow
T'morrow's nothing, to be blunt
You can shove it where you want!

Tips on tomorrow never pay
Tomorrow you'll regret what you did today
And soon enough you'll burn for it as well . . .
So who gives a hoot in hell?

– shove tomorrow where you want!

Blackout. In the darkness the Orchestra plays DON'T BE AFRAID *through the scene change. Lights up on the Salvation Army Mission.*

2

t.l on

The Salvation Army. A mangy Christmas tree. A few of the fold sitting around. Lillian comes in and sits with them. Jane and Hannibal come in with a tureen of soup and start to ladle it out. Jane notices Lillian and points her out to Hannibal.

HANNIBAL: The nerve!

JANE: Comes in and just sits down with the others. I'm going to tell the Major. *She goes into the kitchen.*

HANNIBAL: Unbelievable.

MARY *goes to Lillian*: Miss Holiday, I was told if you ever came back, I should ask you to please leave the premises at once. Major's orders.

LILLIAN: Oh? Give the Major my regards and tell her I am only a poor soul too.

Mary turns to leave in a huff, and meets the Major coming out of the kitchen. She starts to say something, but the Major cuts her off.

MAJOR: So! . . . Well, Holiday, it seems that Bill's Beer Hall wasn't quite right for you either, hm? *Lillian says nothing.* Well, but you really can't stay here, you know.

MARY: She says she's a poor soul too.

MAJOR: Well, she may be a poor soul. But there are some souls we just don't want here.

LILLIAN: I was the best soldier this Army ever had. I knew how to bring God into this – this crummy joint.

Bill comes in, slightly drunk.

MAJOR: And here is another example of the kind of soul we don't want.

BILL: Why, Major, it's Christmas Eve, ain't it? Bless you all, brothers and sisters. You wouldn't turn me out on a night like this – not when I'm just getting interested in what you got to offer.

MAJOR: Mr. Cracker –

LILLIAN: Of course you can stay, Bill.

MAJOR: I think that's quite enough from you, Miss Holiday.

LILLIAN: I don't think it's enough at all, Major. I don't think anything in this room is enough. What is the matter with you people? Where are your minds? There's supposed to be more joy in Heaven over one sinner's repentance than over a thousand righteous men. Here's an important sinner – and all you can give him is a cold shoulder on Christmas Eve!

MAJOR: I'm afraid, Miss Holiday, that Mr. Cracker isn't here tonight to help us pass out the Christmas presents. I don't know why he *is* here, but I know I don't want him here, or you, or the rest of his gang, so if you will kindly – *She is interrupted by the gang swaggering in.*

SAM: Merry Christmas, everybody!

MAJOR: Gentlemen, what can we do for you?

BABY FACE: We just thought we'd stop by and see how the festivities was getting along.

REVEREND: Say, that's a handsome tree, isn't it, Professor?

PROFESSOR: Sheds like a sick Pekinese!

LILLIAN: Gentlemen. I'm truly delighted to see you all here. We had a feeling you'd come, didn't we, Major? And now I think we can start our meeting.

BABY FACE: Hold it, sister. Ya see, the real reason we come by was to find a friend of ours that we ain't seen in a long time. *He goes to Bill, who has unobtrusively wandered off into a corner.* We missed you a lot tonight, buddy boy.

BILL: Missed me?

REVEREND: Where you there?

BILL: Sure!

PROFESSOR: You didn't answer when I signalled.

BILL: Sore throat.

SAM: So where's the swag?

BILL: The what?

SAM: The loot. The haul.

BILL: Oh, that. Right here.

He moves towards his gun pocket. The gang move towards theirs.

LILLIAN *stepping in between the gang and Bill*: Leave Mr. Cracker alone! He's come a long way in the last few hours. On his spiritual journey, I mean.

BILL: Sure, kid, sure.

BABY FACE: That's real nice, Sister. But he ain't got too much further to go. So you better start thinking about a special prayer to say for him tonight, 'cause the next part of his trip is the hardest.

Sam, who has gone over to the window during this, lets out a shrill whistle.

SAM: Cheese it, the cops!

Enter the Cop.

COP: All right, you guys. Suppose you explain to me just what you was doing in the vicinity of the Manufacturer's National Bank this evening? You first.

SAM: Me, officer? I took a drive out to Forest Park tonight. Yellow Cab. Ask the driver.

COP: And I suppose you got his number?

SAM: Sure, 352 –

COP: Skip it. You?

PROFESSOR: Hinky Dink Saloon, all evening, playing poker. Just ask Tessie Miller.

COP: Sure, sure. And you two?

BABY FACE: We was at a inanimate birthday party.

REVEREND: At Captains Wolf's.

BABY FACE, REVEREND *and* COP: Sixty East Oak Street.

COP: They sure do have a lot of birthdays there.

REVEREND: Large family.

BILL *turns around*: Don't you have something to ask me, gumshoe?

COP: Bill Cracker! We've been looking for you. Question of the disappearance of a certain Dr. Nakamura.

LILLIAN: He's innocent, officer, completely innocent!

BILL: C'mon, what good does it do to lie now?

She is stricken.

I want to confess. I did it. I killed Dr. Nakamura.

The door flies open and the Governor walks in. Everyone gasps.

GOVERNOR *sings*:

> If you want to be a big shot
> Start by learning to be tough

BILL *sings*:

> 'Cause you'll never hit the jackpot
> Till you like the going rough.

GOVERNOR:

> All the little shots below you
> Can be blown away like fluff

BILL:

> If they realize when they know you
> That you won't take all their guff

BILL *and* GOVERNOR:

> Just don't get soft, baby
> For God's sake never get soft, baby
> Just keep on pounding him right where it hurts the
>   most
> And if a little shot's big noise should cause a bother
> Don't let if get you down, I mean you're not his father.
>
> Just don't get soft, baby
> For God's sake never get soft, baby

No ifs or buts
Go on and kick him in the guts
Go on and kick him in the guts.

LILLIAN: Governor!

GOVERNOR: Miss Holiday, I am not dead! I had only a slight wound, and the Canal outside is not so very deep. It was simple.

COP: All these crimes! But everybody is innocent!
Church bells begin to toll midnight.

LILLIAN: I think this calls for a celebration! Merry Christmas, everyone!

EVERYONE *ad lib*: Merry Christmas!
The Fly appears at the upstairs window, her gun drawn.

FLY: Not that merry after all, my friends. Bill Cracker, your time is up.
The gang, including the Governor, draw their weapons and aim at Bill.

LILLIAN: Stop! Don't let it happen now!

FLY: Too late, dearie. Two-timers don't get no second chance. Ready, boys?

HANNIBAL *screams*: Sadie!

FLY *seeing him, screams also*: Hannibal!

HANNIBAL: Darling!

FLY: My long lost husband! *She sings:*

When our childhood's warmth was banished
We were warmed in lovers' arms
And we thought that warmth had vanished
Like our childhood's fading charms

HANNIBAL *and* FLY *embracing:*

But the sound of church bells tolling
Through our pain and our dismay

So inspiring, so consoling
It has brought us here today!

LILLIAN *watching them embrace*: Well, Bill, I think it's time you and I got engaged.

BILL: Hold on! I have to think about that for a second.

FLY *to Hannibal*: And I have a small fortune to offer you.

HANNIBAL *taking the bank loot from her*: Why there must be over –

HANNIBAL *and* GANG: – fifty thousand dollars!

HANNIBAL: – in here. Where did you get it all?

FLY: Sewing, night after lonely night.

COP *starting for the sack*: Wait a minute . . .

HANNIBAL: I wouldn't know what to do with all this. *Gives the bag to the Major just as the Cop reaches him.* Major here, for the good of the cause, in honour of my dear Sadie's return.

MAJOR: Accepted gladly, brother!

COP *outmanoeuvred*: Shucks!

LILLIAN: Time's up!

BILL: Awright, I accept.

They embrace. On a signal from the Major, Mary hurries into the kitchen and brings a uniform back to Lillian.

MAJOR: Sister Lillian! It's yours again. This is all your work!

LILLIAN: My old uniform! *As she puts it on:* Just think, Bill, soon you'll be getting one, too! Our work starts tomorrow.

BILL: Well, I dunno . . .

Affectionate laughter. The gang has been conferring, and the Reverend now comes over to Lillian.

REVEREND: Miss Holiday – I beg pardon for interrupting – do you think we all might be able to join your little gang – uh, group?

LILLIAN: What? You mean you all want to repent?

SAM: Well, you see, Miss, our line of work has suddenly gotten very uninteresting.

PROFESSOR: We've decided we want to be more useful to the world.

LILLIAN: That's the spirit! Major?

MAJOR *who has been gazing into the moneybag*: I'm astounded! Mr. Wurlitzer, I'm now in a position to accept your organ.

SAM *embracing her*: Field Marshal, you're a darling!

MAJOR: Why – I don't know what to say!

FLY: Then let me say it for you! Our two groups have been fighting the same enemy all along. It's time to forget our little quarrels and stand together. Blasting open a safe is nothing – we've got to blast open the big gang that keeps the safe locked. So slip on your brass knuckles and learn where to hit! Robbing a bank's no crime compared to owning one! The world belongs to all of us – let's march together and make it our own!

ALL: Hurray!

LILLIAN *sings*:

> Look all around you
> Look all around you
> Look all around you, we see you're about to drown!
> We hear you screaming 'Help me!'
> We'll catch you before you fall down
> Stop all the traffic now, let's clear the air
> You who need help, keep your hopes up, we're here and
> > we care
> Your souls can still be saved
> But hear us, hear us, brother, before you reach the
> > grave
>
> Though troubles may beset you
> We swear we won't forget you
> Though now you stand in need
> Though now you stand in need

Don't tell us, 'Things will stay the way they are now'.
This unjust world will never be the same

EVERYONE:

If all of you will swear to stand together
Forget your fears and march with us today
So bring on the tanks and the cannon
And squadrons of planes let there be
And battleships on the sea

LILLIAN:

Just to conquer one small bowl of soup for every
poor man
Just to conquer one small bowl of soup for every
poor man

EVERYONE:

Let every man come join us
Our purpose to ensure
The army that is great and strong
Is the army of the poor

LILLIAN:

Forward march, chin up, take weapons, prepare!
You who need help, keep your hopes up, we're coming,
we care!

One last title on the screen: THE HAPPY END.